The working w

A practical and readable handbook w...... .... ,
gain satisfaction and success at work.

The Working woman's guide

A unique compendium of every
aspect of your working life

by

Liz Hodgkinson

THORSONS PUBLISHERS LIMITED
Wellingborough, Northamptonshire

First published 1985

© LIZ HODGKINSON 1985

British Library Cataloguing in Publication Data

Hodgkinson, Liz
    The working woman's guide: a unique
    compendium of every aspect of your working life.
    1. Women – Employment – Great Britain
    2. Women – Training of – Great Britain
    I. Title
    331.7'02'0941   HD6135

ISBN 0-7225-0980-4

Printed and bound in Great Britain

Contents

Introduction

There is nothing new about women working. From the dawn of history, women have worked quite as hard as men. Generations upon generations have toiled in the house and on the land, often without stopping except to snatch a few hours' sleep at night.

But that sort of work could hardly be regarded as a career. Most of the work women did in the past was essential labour, enabling them and their families to stay alive. It was relentless slog, carried out for sheer survival, rather than being a job done out of sheer enjoyment of the task.

What is fairly new is the idea that women should be able to choose for themselves a proper, satisfying, lifelong career – other than running a home and bringing up a family, that is. Until the 1950s, most women regarded the paid work they did as a stopgap between school and marriage. Now, the female expectation of working life has been extended to cover the time up till the birth of the first baby. Then, often long after their families have been completed, some women start thinking about going back to some kind of paid employment.

There *are* many dedicated career women, of course, as there have been for the past hundred years. But, even in the 'eighties, they are still not in the majority. For all too many women, work outside the home tends to be seen as peripheral, rather than their 'real' job, which takes place mainly inside the home.

Women's work is still regarded very differently from men's. On the whole, men expect to have an unbroken career pattern from the time they leave school or college until they retire. They may change jobs, of course, and even, on occasion, completely change direction, but mostly they reckon to be earning for the greater part of their adult lives.

This difference in attitude means that men tend to get the best jobs, and women have to take the more menial, less well-paid ones that the men don't want.

'Women's work' in history
Before the industrial revolution of the mid-nineteenth century, both men and women worked very near the home. In 1750, two out of every three people lived a mainly agricultural life and such jobs as there were

would be confined to tilling the soil or looking after farm animals. Women in those days did essential work to keep body and soul together, such as weaving, spinning, sewing, looking after the dairy, cooking and baking. In those days very few men, let alone women, thought about what we would call a career. You simply did exactly the same as your parents and grandparents before you.

Even in the upper reaches of society there were not many real careers on offer. A man could be a soldier, writer or politician, and the most an ambitious woman could hope for was to be the mistress of some great man. Almost the only profession – apart from the oldest one – available to women before the nineteenth century, was that of writing. And often this had to be done in great secret, or under an assumed – usually male – name.

Women did not, in those days, have many statutory rights and were treated very much as their husband's property, whatever their social standing might be. The pattern of life changed for ever during the technological developments of the Victorian era when, for the first time, droves of people went out to work. Women were very much needed in the early days of the revolution, and worked as coal miners and factory hands alongside the men. From the start, though, they were paid less than the male workers, even when the jobs were identical.

Those who owned the factories, and grew rich on the sweated labour of their exploited employees, saw the ultimate pinacle of success as being able to keep a wife in luxury and idleness at home. Work for women was then seen as something only for the poorer classes, because they simply had no choice in the matter.

As technological advances proceeded, so did the professions. The nineteenth century saw the emergence of the professions as we now know them. Doctors, lawyers, architects, civil servants, became organized and formal exams were held before young men could be admitted to the ranks. Schools proliferated – for boys. The rich or professional man's wife and daughters lived in parasitic splendour, and were denied any opportunity to follow a proper profession for themselves. They were expected to be content with a little embroidery, piano playing and drawing – the so-called 'accomplishments' – and were lucky if they were educated beyond a very elementary level.

In 1850, 30 per cent of the workforce was female, but the idea was growing, among men at least, that in a perfect world, women should not need to earn their bread at all. Most women's jobs in those days were very low-grade, of course. In 1861, four-fifths of women who were working were employed in domestic service or the textile industry.

In 1884, Factory Acts, trying to be humanitarian, excluded women from working night shifts, and limited their working hours to twelve a day. Those women working in tedious menial jobs because they came from poor families, used to sit at their looms and dream that they would entrap some rich man and never have to work again. Few did, of course.

But at the same time, some of the more middle-class women were realizing that work of the right sort could actually enhance their lives and give them greater purpose and challenge. There have always been women who rebelled against the status quo of their day, but somehow nothing very much happened to improve female career conditions until about a hundred years ago. Then, some intelligent women who had been going quietly mad at home decided to campaign for the right to education and a profession, as well as money of their own.

A few of the more far-sighted realized that marriage, children and a life of choosing dresses and visiting other ladies in similar materially comfortable circumstances, need not be all that life could offer. Why, they asked, could a man become a lawyer, a minister of religion, go to public school and receive a university education when all these were denied to girls? Surely it couldn't be that girls were less intelligent than boys?

That had been the assumption, of course. But as soon as it was put to the test, everybody began to realize that girls had brains, too. The trouble was that, as soon as they were allowed to take exams, they disturbed all the males by coming top. This would never do at all. The only way to make sure women stayed in their proper, subordinate place was to exclude them from the professions, by law.

So this was done. Women were not allowed to enter medical schools, or the universities. They were not allowed to practise as barristers or solicitors, even if they passed all their law exams. They were barred from taking Civil Service exams. But one by one, as pressure from women built up, and citadels were stormed, these laws were relaxed. Gradually, by sheer campaigning on their own behalf, women succeeded in gaining admittance to universities, obtaining degrees and entering the professions.

Equality in the eighties?

Yet all this took place years and years ago. It is well over a hundred years since the first women doctors were allowed to practice, and almost 60 years since women were allowed to vote on exactly the same terms as men. It is nearly 70 years since the first woman MP, Nancy Astor, took up her seat in the House of Commons.

So why, in the eighties, do we still have only two dozen women MPs, and why do women make up only 20 per cent of the practising medical profession? Why are only nine per cent of the country's managers women? Why are 98 per cent of all directors men? Why are there still no women in the very top grades of the civil service? Why are there no women Anglican ministers? No female diplomats? No women editors of national newspapers?

Because, maybe, less has changed than we like to think. It is true that the Equal Pay Act of 1970 and the Sex Discrimination Act five years later, were attempts to remove the last traces of inequality standing in the way of a woman and her career.

Yet enormous inequalities still remain. The fight is by no means won. Marriage is still seen as very much more of a career for women than it is for men. There is a thriving magazine called *Brides*, but there is not a similar one called *Bridegrooms*. Nobody thinks any the less of a woman who decides to relinquish her own career so that she can become a full-time wife and mother. The paid work women do is still considered very much less important than the paid work men do. Countless speeches, impassioned pleas and thousands of words have done little to alter this state of affairs.

Girls are now, at long last, educated in much the same way as boys but, even though girls are usually encouraged to take up careers, there remains the feeling that a girl's career is less central to her life. I still meet parents who are quite prepared to pay for their sons to go to independent schools, but are happy for their daughters to attend the local, free, comprehensive. If there is money to send only one child, the boy is most often the recipient.

Daughters, rather than sons, are expected to be available, giving up their jobs if necessary, to look after elderly relatives or young children. Wives are expected to follow their husbands wherever their careers might take them, but you hardly ever hear of a husband following a wife. It is so rare that, when it does happen, it makes news.

There are now few formal legal obstacles standing in the way of a woman and her career, but there are forces at work far stronger than mere legislative ones. There is all the force of tradition and habit. It is undeniable that, in spite of all that has been done on their behalf, women still aren't achieving high positions in their careers. Many are too ready to give up before they have climbed even a quarter of the way up the ladder.

There are glorious exceptions, of course. But they tend to be the exceptions that prove the rule. But, why are there not large numbers of women at the top of the professions? Why are virtually all professional people still *men*?

Are women not succeeding because the outside world is still too masculine a place for them? Are the professions still run too much like a man's club, where women are admitted only on sufferance? Perhaps women are by nature more timid, dependent, passive and less assertive and dominant than men. Could this be the reason why they are not succeeding?

The arguments can go on and on, round and round. Meanwhile, very little seems to alter. I don't propose to go into all the arguments, whys and wherefores, as this book is intended to be a practical guide. But you need to know what the obstacles are, before you can begin to overcome them.

Planning for the future

I do believe that every woman nowadays is entitled to a proper career, independence, and a lifestyle which does not have to be supported by another's income.

I also believe that girls have to start thinking about, and preparing for, their future careers at a very early age, say 13 or 14. This does not necessarily mean knowing exactly what you want to do, but having the attitude that you will remain an independently-operating human being for all of your life.

It is no longer any use – if indeed it ever was – expecting a dashing young romantic hero to come along, love you for ever and lavish you with all you could desire. No human being has the power to ensure happiness for another and men are no stronger, emotionally, than women. On a more practical note, it is by no means certain, if you do marry such a hero, that he will stay with you for life, or that you will want to stay with him. Around 300,000 women in Britain alone now get divorced every year, and these can manage much better if they have proper careers they can continue. The whole procedure becomes so much less shattering if you can support yourself financially. Those who have built up a life for themselves are less dumfounded when relationships come to an end.

But it is a paradoxical truth that, the more equal you are, the more independent, the more chance your marriage has of surviving and succeeding. A relationship that is built on mutual respect can endure many storms.

Nowadays, it is the career girls who have the best chance of meeting the most exciting men. And men themselves are starting to prefer career women as lifetime partners, as they find them more exciting and stimulating. So, if a lasting relationship is what you desire, you have everything to gain and nothing at all to lose from carving out a career for yourself.

This is not to say that everybody is equally gifted, equally motivated and equally dedicated. After all, not all men are career-minded. But now the chance is there for you, and it is up to you to take it. Only you can give yourself a good career, and only you can make it work. But it's not always easy to know how to go about achieving a satisfying working life, and that is one of the main reasons why this book has been written.

Women will never have good careers until they can start to take their working lives absolutely seriously. This means not drifting along in the hope that something will turn up. It won't, unless you make it. Fate needs a helping hand from time to time. When the lucky break does occur – and these do happen occasionally for everybody – you have to be ready to take advantage of it.

I advocate lifelong careers for women because I know that life becomes so much more exciting and rewarding if you have a good job to go to. Of course, there can be satisfaction in running a home and having a family, but modern homes are so easy to run and most families so small these days, that this can hardly be called a career in itself any longer. Women who have careers stay younger, happier, healthier and have a more positive outlook generally than those who are bored, but stay at home. Such women are also less likely to bring up children with dependent attitudes.

It is also true that you do need quite a strong dose of courage to get yourself launched onto a career path. The going will be tough at times, and the higher you set your sights, the more thorny your path will become. There may well be times when you wonder whether it's all worth it, but it is.

Remember, that all the laws which govern our existence were passed by men. This will never change until there are lots more women all the way up the ladder. You won't change the world by scuttling back home the minute the going gets tough.

First and foremost, having a lasting career depends on securing a good education. And there is no excuse not to be well trained these days. Even if you missed out at school – and there are signs that the move towards coeducation is having an adverse effect on girls – there are all sorts of schemes on offer all over the country. And you don't have to be rich to take advantage of them. Many courses for mature women are completely free, or give a generous grant while training.

The better trained you are, the more your market value improves. In general, women are still confined to the lowest paid jobs in the country, and this is mainly because they have no special training or skills to offer.

In spite of all that may be said to the contrary, you don't have to give up your career to bring up a family. You can if you like, of course, as there is no law that says you *have* to work if you don't want to. But even if you do stop working outside the home for a few years, there is nothing to prevent you getting back to a good job. The secret is to build having a family into your career structure – not to stop work and then, some years later, wonder how on earth you will ever get back to your previous position.

The important thing to realize is that you don't have to settle for less than the best, simply because of your sex. We are often told that there are no childcare provisions, and that this is why women cease to work when they have families. But there *are* provisions. They may not be perfect, but they exist and they can be improved. You don't have to earn a fortune and pay a top-class nanny all your wages, just in order to keep working. There are other, perfectly good, answers to the childcare problem for women at all income levels. Why aren't women getting together and starting nurseries that fit in with proper working hours? It's no use waiting for 'them' to provide 24-hour nurseries. A day nursery could become a very nice little business in itself for women who like having children around them.

Lives of great women all remind us that we *can* have good careers, that we *can* earn good money, and that we *can* climb to the top of the career ladder. Whenever resolution falters, keep in mind all those women who have achieved, often in spite of tremendous odds. Don't ever hear yourself saying: it's all right for her, she's had more chances than I have.

The truth is, everybody gets a chance. But it's up to you what you make of it.

1

School and College

Do you choose a career, or does a career choose you? If you have a burning desire to be a singer, actress, writer or missionary, and are determined that nothing, but nothing, will stop you, then the answer is probably the latter. Most of the world's geniuses have been people who were completely unable to resist the pull of their particular vocation. It was always something that seemed far stronger than they were, which they felt powerless to resist.

Most people, of course, do not fall into this category. The vast majority of girls – and boys too, for that matter – go through school and college with no very definite idea of what they want to do in life. Many students haven't even got a very clear idea after graduating from university. After all, there are now around 4,500 different careers to choose from. How do you go about picking the one that is exactly right for you?

How do you plan a career path? How do you get to the top? What is 'the top' anyway? What if you decide to have a family? This book will attempt to deal with all these questions, and provide some answers for all girls and women who expect to work and remain economically independent for the rest of their lives. And today that is a growing number of us. The days when we could reasonably expect a man to keep us, are now well and truly over. According to a recent survey carried out by the Equal Opportunities Commission, only five per cent of households in this country currently have a male head, with a dependent wife, and two dependent children.

But apart from any considerations of economic necessity, life becomes so much more fun if you have a career that you can call your own. To be independent, self-reliant and busy – these are the goals that every woman should aim at, for they are the secrets of success, inner strength, health, happiness, and long-lasting youth.

This book does not contain a specific careers guide, as there are plenty of excellent such books already on the market, which list all the qualifications, experience and background you need to pursue a particular career. Anyone who is wondering exactly which profession might be the one for her should read all of these books avidly, as they mention possibilities you may not have even considered.

Think ahead
It is essential that girls should realize, from early teenagehood on, that it is vital for them to think in terms of having a career which will be satisfying and right, and one which can develop, change and mature along with the person. This doesn't necessarily mean rejecting careers which, on the face of it, seem short-lived. If you are pretty, tall and extremely slim you may consider a career as a model, and your teachers and parents may instantly try to dissuade you, pointing out that this job lasts only a few years and that hardly any girls ever make it anyway.

But the job of a model can, in itself, open up exciting new vistas which can lead to a more permanent career long after your face has ceased to be your fortune. In the old days girls used to become models so that they could hook rich husbands, but now many girls are finding that modelling can lead to other, longer-lasting careers, in photography, writing or the business world.

Former model Laraine Ashton now runs her own model agency, ex-model Pat Booth is a photographer and writer, Lorraine Chase is an actress, and Debbie Moore an astute business woman with her thriving Pineapple Dance Studios.

I'm not suggesting that girls should reject proper careers in favour of modelling, but pointing out that capitalizing on a pretty face when you are young does not have to condemn you to years of inaction in later life.

Having a good career does not mean that you must know from the age of eight exactly what you want to do, and then direct all your energies towards attaining that end. But it does mean that, throughout your school and college days, you should have a serious and dedicated attitude towards work, and never expect that somebody else will always be there to provide the wherewithal for a good life.

Women in the professions
Some of you, reading this chapter so far, may say, but haven't we been through all this before? Surely, girls have achieved equal status and opportunities, and the world of careers is now wide open to them. It is true that, in theory at least, there is nothing to stop any female from becoming a doctor, lawyer, architect, prime minister even. There are now no universities in Britain at least and few courses that are barred to women. Almost the only profession that still insists on men only is the Anglican ministry, and even that bastion is bound to fall before long. So hasn't the battle already been fought and won?

At first glance, this may certainly seem to be so. At present around 40 per cent of undergraduates at Oxford are female, and half the intake at medical schools is also female. Twenty years ago, the quota was a quarter of female students. We now have women judges and company directors, and female millionaires in their own right.

So can't we all sit back and relax now? No, not at all, because a closer look at the figures shows that, in reality, women are very far from being well represented at the top in most of the professions. A few make it, sure, but the latest figures show that, in the medical world for example, over 80 per cent of GPs and over 90 per cent of consultants are male.

In the Civil Service, which prides itself on being an exceptionally liberal-minded equal employer, we find that, at the very top, there are hardly any women at all. This point was amusingly driven home in the popular comedy series, *Yes Minister*. James Hacker, Minister for Administrative Affairs, asks his smooth, bland Permanent Secretary, Sir Humphrey Appleby, just how many women there are in his (Sir Humphrey's) position. 'Without looking at the figures I couldn't say exactly, Minister,' he hedges. 'Roughly speaking,' persists Hacker. 'Roughly speaking, er Minister?' Sir Humphrey pretends to think. 'Roughly speaking – er, none.'

The figures do not increase significantly further down the scale. In 1983, there were just four women Deputy Secretaries and 22 women Under Secretaries, less than four per cent of the total in each case.

You may point out that you don't want to be a Civil Servant anyway, and you don't really care how many women Permanent Secretaries there are. But a glance at all the other professions which require a high level of training reveal that the position is very little different anywhere. In local government, only one woman out of a total of one and three-quarter million employees has risen to the position of chief executive.

Women at the top
Around nine per cent of those currently holding managerial positions in this country are women. At the BBC, another supposedly liberal-minded employer, granting generous maternity leave and prepared to consider job-sharing schemes, we discover that they have just one per cent of women in the very top 'A' grade jobs. And only fifteen per cent of those in managerial positions at the mighty Beeb are women. How many controllers are there of the various TV stations? How many women head radio networks? None, at a national level, though there are one or two women managing directors in local radio.

The Greater London Council, which grants many thousands of pounds every year to women's schemes and has a woman's equality officer, Valerie Wise, does not have even one principal female architect in its employment. Though 40 per cent of architecture undergraduates are now female, the GLC's total number of women architects, in all grades, is less than 10 per cent.

In other jobs, the overall picture looks just as depressing. Around one per cent of chartered surveyors are women, five per cent of chartered accountants are female, 0.2 of production engineers, and eleven per cent of lawyers. According to a new survey carried out by *Director* magazine, only two per cent of Britain's 250,000 directors are women. The magazine said: 'The sight of a woman in the boardroom is rare enough. The sight of one in the Managing Director's chair is as exotic as a pair of nesting ospreys.'

Though many women train as teachers and, indeed, teaching has long been regarded as a woman's job *par excellence*, they are mainly concentrated in the primary and junior school levels. As one goes higher up the educational spiral, fewer and fewer women are found. Hardly any women are head teachers of mixed comprehensives, and more men are now becoming heads of primary schools. Only one per cent of university professors in this country are women. Both here and in America, around 12 per cent of the total academic staff at university is composed of women. Yet, over 99 per cent of infant school teachers are women. Seventy-seven per cent of primary school teachers are women, and 44 per cent of secondary school teachers.

Whenever we encounter The Top, we find it heavily weighted down with men. The situation is not much more hopeful for jobs in the arts. If you see six women members of a major orchestra, it looks a lot. How many women leading conductors are there? How many women directors of art galleries, how many women are famous painters? How many women creative directors are there in the big advertising agencies?

We find little deviation from this pattern in all the career-type jobs, even in these days of 'equal opportunities'. In her hard-hitting book *Danger – Men at Work*, polytechnic lecturer Rosalind Miles points out that though there are now over 10 million working women in this country, compared to five million female earners in 1911, we are still overwhelmingly concentrated in the lowly and badly-paid jobs.

Why is this? Is it because women are basically less clever and career-minded than men? Or is there some other reason why women are still failing to achieve in the outside world? Would more women get to the top if we weren't the ones left holding the babies?

To all these questions, one has to answer both yes and no. In all intelligence tests women seem to do as well as men and yet, on the whole, more men gain high professional qualifications. More women would, undoubtedly, get to the top if they didn't bear and look after the children. But yet, nearly all of the women who have attained the pinnacle have had children. Look at Margaret Thatcher, Golda Meir, Indira Gandhi, Esther Rantzen, gynaecologist Dame Josephine Barnes – all are or were mothers as well as high-flying career women. Children may be a factor, but they are by no means the whole reason for women's comparative lack of success in the working world. Could it be, then, that we are born without that vital spark of determination and persistence that would take us far?

Teenage influences

Without wishing to enter into all the arguments about nature and nurture, for the moment at least, one could say that conditioning and role models do provide at least part of the answer. One continuing problem is that, at the critical age of 13 or 14, many girls start becoming interested in boys, make-up and clothes. They read comic strip papers which glorify the girl-meets-boy answer to all problems in life.

Girls at an early age gain the impression that the most important things in life are to have thick shiny hair, a size 10 figure and a pretty face that will attract the boys. And boys, it is well known, don't like girls who are too clever, as it shows them up and destroys their developing egos at a tender age. All the teenage comics still underline that message.

It is still the case that, in coeducational schools, girls tend to drop out of maths and science at exactly the same age as they start to become interested in boys. Up to the age of 11 or 12, they remain far ahead of boys in academic excellence and achievement. They also tend to be harder working and more competitive at school. Then, mysteriously, they start to tail off and drop out of academic competition, allowing the boys to steam ahead. Suddenly, maths and physics are seen as 'hard' subjects, unfeminine, and unsuitable for girls who, only a year or two before, were at the very top of their class in these subjects.

Girls now pass as many O-levels as boys, but in completely different subjects. Around one quarter of all female O-level candidates take physics, and 30 per cent take chemistry. Only three per cent take technical drawing, whereas 98 per cent of cookery candidates are female. And there's another tale. Though most cookery enthusiasts at school are female, it's the men who end up being head chefs at five-star hotels.

At A-level, the scenario looks even more divisive. Nineteen per cent of girls take A-level physics, and 25 per cent take maths, whereas at this level, 99.9 per cent of the passes in domestic subjects are gained by girls.

Now, I'm not saying that O- and A-level passes in maths or physics are an automatic passport to worldly success. Far from it. But I am pointing out that there is a definite tendency for girls to limit their options at a very early age indeed. Girls don't stop taking maths and science subjects because they are unable to do them: they give them up because they stop having confidence in their ability to achieve.

They start thinking of themselves as second rate citizens, or at least, second rate pupils. And unfortunately, teachers often unwittingly collude in this. In her book *Invisible Women: The Schooling Scandal*, Australian writer Dale Spender noticed that, in any coeducational class of teenagers, boys were always given more time and attention than girls. Dale Spender, when herself a teacher, thought this was dreadful and decided that no such discrimination would occur in her lessons. So she made sure she gave the girls extra attention – or thought she did. But when Dale made tapes of herself teaching she discovered that she, too, gave the boys extra time *while fully believing that she was focusing mainly on the girls*. This, she feels, is a potent argument against coeducation. In mixed schools, she notes, girls tend to do badly, because they are competing for the boys' attention, rather than good marks.

I witnessed this for myself in a mixed secondary school in Sussex, where I once interviewed teachers and 14-year-old girls, for a newspaper article. The maths teacher there said that he had to bully the girls, almost, into taking maths at O-level. He agreed that they dropped out simply because there were boys in the class and suddenly, maths seemed unfeminine.

This particular teacher had a high pass rate for girls at O-level maths, largely because he had a powerful and persuasive personality, and half the O-level class each year fell in love with him, so the other teachers informed me. Not, perhaps, the ideal way to persuade girls to continue with their education, but it shows how all-persuasive is this emphasis on love and romance for young girls. In this case, of course – but not very often – the end justified the means!

Times have changed little in this respect since the last century when Miss Dorothea Beale and Miss Frances Buss, founder of Cheltenham Ladies' College, and the North London Collegiate School for girls, were lampooned in this rhyme:

> Miss Buss and Miss Beale
> Cupid's darts do not feel.
> How different from us
> Miss Beale and Miss Buss.

Academically speaking, girls do better at all girls' schools. There is no doubt whatever of this. Boys on the other hand, do better at mixed schools, as they feel in direct competition with the girls, and want to show them how clever they are. So it is not a good thing for girls' education that the moves are for more and more coed schools, and for leading boys' public schools to take girls into the sixth form. At one boys' school, Westminster, there is terrific competition for sixth form places for girls. The excellent academic record is only one reason why girls want to leave their former all-girls' schools and go there – the glamour and appeal of being in a mainly boys' school is very strong. One Westminster girl pupil told me that the standard of her work had definitely gone down since entering the sixth form there, and she had to make a special effort to pull up again when she realized what was happening.

The opposite does not apply, and there is little rush from boys for places at predominantly girls' schools. Too early, even in the 1980s, girls start thinking of themselves to be admired only for their physical attributes, rather than for their mental powers or perception.

This is a short-lived and dangerous attitude, as it leads so often to misery and frustration in later life. Unfortunately, the lure of physical attractiveness is one that is very hard to resist. When I was at school it was the pretty girls, rather than the cleverest or wisest, who were most admired. Those who were good at maths or physics were not only not admired, they were actually looked down on. Yes, we all said as we applied yet another surreptitious layer of mascara, she may get 99 per cent for maths, but would you like to look like her?

We felt it was far more important to achieve just that correct height of beehive hairdo, to have a pair of white stilettos, all to attain that ultimate accolade of attractive girlhood – a boyfriend on one's arm. Real status was to be seen walking hand in hand with a boy.

One friend of mine, now a high-powered newspaper executive, thinks back with shame to the days when, as a very pretty 16-year-old, she was asked by a potential boyfriend how many O-levels she had. Judging correctly that he probably hadn't done very well, she replied without batting her long eyelashes: three. In fact, she had nine O-level passes, many at grade A.

Well, all right, that was in 1962. But have things changed much since then? No, not really. In fact, they've hardly changed at all. Girls still tend to compete, not so much for high honours in the academic world, as for the regard of a boyfriend. We haven't quite got over the attitude that, in order to be 'feminine', a girl must also be dim. More than a few remnants of that outdated and limiting standpoint remain.

Role models

Another reason for girls continuing to take second place in jobs is that, looking round, they see so few of their sex in truly authoritative positions. If you don't actually see very many women at the top, you can easily come to the conclusion that they are somehow incapable of being there.

Very many girls see their mothers as basically housewives, with perhaps a small part-time job, and certainly earning much less than their fathers. At school, they see men as headmasters, and senior teachers. When they go to the doctor, they are more than likely to be seen by a man. It is very easy to pick up the impression that the outside world is not a woman's place, and that you may as well give up the fight, look decorative, and relegate yourself to eternal second best.

People learn more from what they observe than from what they are told, and if girls everywhere see women in subordinate positions, they can't help gaining the impression that this is where they are meant to be. The male boss has a female secretary, the male doctor has a female receptionist, the male lawyer has a female legal secretary. It is unfortunate that so much of this subordination sets in in the early teenage years in the mistaken name of love. Though we may grow out of this later, and indeed most of us do, by that stage it could be rather late to extricate oneself from a dependent, lowly position and embark on a good career. The time to start thinking seriously about your working life is long before O-level decisions have been made.

Work should be fun

If girls tell themselves that they can expect to work, and do not see themselves being supported by somebody else, this attitude will in itself help to determine sensible career choices. There can be no possible argument about it. Having your own career, your own individual role and niche in society, is a far better way to live than sitting at home all day waiting for a man to return from work. 'Work is more fun than fun', said American *Cosmopolitan's* editor Helen Gurley Brown, and how right she was. There is no greater satisfaction in life than the frisson that comes from working at a job you really enjoy.

It doesn't always have to be particularly high powered, or fantastically well paid, to be satisfying and rewarding. But, in order to give you confidence and that vital feeling of self esteem, any job you do must contain two ingredients. It must be able to stretch you to the limits of your creativity and intelligence, and it must be a continual challenge.

You must be able to say, that if a fairy godmother could come and grant you any wish you liked, there is nothing in the world you would rather be doing than your job. I can't really over-emphasize this point – working at a fulfilling job is better for you than all the vitamin pills and health farms and holidays in the world. It is being busy and useful in a good job that keeps women healthy, active and attractive. Boredom and that feeling that you are living vicariously, are the greatest agers, health destroyers and energy-sappers there are.

Careers advice

Certainly, women have made significant strides. The other day I picked up a book of careers for girls written in 1955. The author, Jeanne Heal, a famous television personality of her day, began her book thus: 'Since it is agreed that most girls want a husband, a home and a family, and regard a job as a stopgap between leaving school and getting married, what is the case for women entering the professions?' She goes on: 'To me, the basic feeling of being independent, of being able to earn my own income given even the nicest husband in the world to keep me, is an absolute essential. But I know that my outlook is far from typical. I know that most women prefer not to have a job, and I know there are intelligent reasons why being a housewife and a mother can be the most satisfying wholetime job in the world.'

Thirty years later, I suspect few authors writing about careers for girls would feel the need to be so apologetic about their standpoint. I imagine it is agreed nowadays that most women *do* want a job, and would prefer to work. But so often they just can't see their way clear to doing it, and fitting a good career in with the more traditional female roles. Even today, if you pick up the average career book, the differences between male and female commitment are still made.

One excellent book, *First Steps to a Career*, by Kalyani Menon, published in 1981, states in its introduction: 'Now that it is usual for women to go on working after they are married and have families, you may be thinking about careers that can be done on a part-time basis.'

The author very sensibly goes on to say that no career should ever be chosen purely for its convenient hours, but the very words 'part-time' somehow seep into a woman's soul at a very early age. The words themselves imply a less than total commitment, and without total commitment you are never going to get far in any job you may do.

There is still a very strong assumption, driven home in many schools and by countless careers teachers, that while a man must have an unbroken career pattern, it is quite all right for a woman's to be more fragmented. Advice on careers for girls always covers the question: will I be able to return to it later, after taking a break to have a family? Men never seem to have to ask themselves the same question.

What I'm saying is that the assumption that women's careers are somehow less vital, less central to their lives and more of a sideline or little indulgence, something to be picked up and dropped at will, tends to limit a girl's choices even before she starts. If, at the age of 13, you are told that you must think about taking a break to have children, and then return at some later date, possibly part-time, or at a lower level, the message will inevitably colour your views about your career, and working life. It can soon become an automatic assumption that you must take this possibility on board.

That is, I know, the reality today. From my vantage point I can see very many women, now in their thirties, who did not, as teenagers, take their careers at all seriously.

They assumed, as so many of us did in those days, that it didn't much matter if we didn't succeed, as we didn't want to be butch and masculine anyway, and men preferred women who didn't display too much aggressive intelligence. When you are in your thirties, you don't really care all that much about what men prefer. But to a 15-year-old, 30 is ancient – you never even think you can reach that advanced age.

The profession of housewife?

Some thinking ahead is essential, though, otherwise you can find yourself rapidly becoming a non-person in the world at large. In her highly controversial book *Sex and Destiny*, Germaine Greer says that many older women who say they want a job are really making a plea to re-enter society. As a housebound housewife dependent on a man's income, you are effectively relegated to non-personhood. The trouble is, if you do decide to re-enter society in your fourth decade, you can find many doors very firmly shut to you. You then realize, with horror, that you have no current experience or qualifications, no job contacts and, most of all, no confidence in yourself. One careers advisor told me that men lose confidence in themselves six months after being made redundant. How much more does a woman lose after being 10 years in the home?

We used to be told, and still are to some extent, that running a home is a responsible, demanding job that requires a high level of managerial skill. Indeed, Mrs Thatcher herself made some such pronouncement not so very long ago. But what can she be thinking of? Did a male speech writer suddenly slip this in while she wasn't looking? Because, whoever tells you this, don't be taken in.

Bringing a family up well is, unarguably, a very important and responsible job, but this does not mean you have to sacrifice everything else in order to do it properly, and stop being an autonomous individual.

Also, when running a home, you can be as lazy or inefficient as you like, and nobody is going to give you the sack, or promote you. There are no tangible rewards, little job satisfaction, and nobody ever says thank you, and means it. If they do, they are probably being patronizing. When running a home, there are no deadlines to meet, no targets to achieve, no goals to attain, and those doing the job of running a home know it. You may be told it's important, but you don't feel very important doing it.

In fact, most often you feel the complete opposite of important. You feel marooned, isolated, and uncared for – adrift in a society that does not, whatever its protestations to the contrary, value the work you do.

Life wasn't always like this of course. In pre-industrial days, when most families were self-sufficient, the wife's weaving, baking and sewing were absolutely essential to keep the home and economy together. Now, a housewife need not ever sew, mend, weed the potato patch or bake a loaf of bread. She can clothe her family and feed them simply by getting out the hatchback and driving to the nearest shopping precinct. So society has changed radically in this respect, and we as women do not need to drudge in order to maintain a comfortable home. Modern homes virtually run themselves.

A recent survey carried out by an insurance firm estimated that the average woman at home with three children spent 80 hours a week on housework. The object of the survey was, of course, to get men to fork out more for life insurance, but even allowing for that bias, many women at home very probably do spend getting on for that length of time on housework. But inanimate things are just not worth all those hours. You could only spend that amount of time doing drudgery if you had nothing much else to do with your time.

You may decide, eventually, that you actually enjoy running a home more than anything else in the world. If that is so, who is to argue with you? It is a very different matter from being 'just a housewife' because there is absolutely nothing else in the world that you can do.

Academic options

In order to give yourself the best possible chance of working at a good career, you need to keep all your academic options open for as long as possible. If you have decided that all you want to do in the world is to be a prima ballerina, then you will have to narrow your options instead, and start to specialize very early in life. But, for nearly all girls, maintaining a wide choice for as long as you can is essential for career success. And that, in the first instance, means taking all the academic O-levels within your range. It does not mean opting instead for 'girls' subjects', because they seem easier, or even opting for 'boys' subjects' simply out of a spirit of rebellion or protest.

One careers analyst, with more than 20 years' experience in the field, maintains that anybody of reasonable intelligence can pass any O-level subjects whatsoever, given the motivation. You do not need special aptitude in a subject to do well at this stage. It is a different matter at A-level, of course. Essential O-levels are: maths, English language and literature, a foreign language, a science, history and/or geography. All others, such as domestic science, art, woodwork, can be regarded as makeweights and not essential, even if you wish to specialize in them later. You do not need an O-level in cookery to pass it at A-level. You are bound to enjoy some subjects more than others, and be better at certain ones, but there is no sex-linked reason why you should not pass them all at this relatively elementary stage.

CSE was introduced about 20 years ago, with the object of ensuring that pupils who were not up to O-levels should leave school with at least a piece of paper to say they had completed 11 years full-time education. It was a worthy aim, no doubt, but it has not achieved much respect in the market place. CSE is regarded, by teachers, parents and employers as a second-class qualification. It is the booby prize of the educational world and as such, should be avoided wherever possible. Most of the leading boys' and girls' public schools in this country do not even entertain the idea of CSEs, except perhaps for craft-type subjects, and quite right too. All their pupils – even the less academically gifted ones – and there are plenty of these at independent schools – must have a go at O-levels. A surprising number of them pass, as well, mainly because it is expected of them. Any girl who is generally clever, but 'not much good' at maths or science, should still aim at the O-level, rather than the CSE, as the latter will mark her down as having no mathematical or scientific ability whatsoever. Aim for the top, even if you have to stage a little fight to do it. Don't ever allow yourself to be shunted off into the CSE class just because you are a girl, or meekly accept your inabilities.

When I was at school, and about to take O-level maths, my teacher informed me that if I were to have six months' tuition, six days a week, for six hours a day, I still wouldn't have a hope in hell of passing. Guess who didn't pass maths O-level? It can be difficult to resist negative prophetic utterances like these, but it is a law of nature that if anyone tells you you are sure to fail, you tend to oblige by doing that very thing.

Anyway, all the agonizing and worrying over whether to take O-levels or CSEs will end in 1986, when the present exam system is to be abolished, and replaced by a single exam, called the GCSE – General Certificate of Secondary Education – taken at age 16. There will still be 'hard' and 'easy' options, but the main idea is to end the divisiveness that has grown up over O-levels and CSEs. The first candidates will actually be sitting for this new exam in 1988.

What about when it comes to A-level? As I said earlier, this is where girls and science subjects tend to part company, usually for ever. There are several reasons why this is so. One is that girls are still, on the whole, not expected to be good at science, and the self-fulfilling prophecy mentioned earlier operates in full force. Another reason is that of the role-model mentality. Girls at the still impressionable age of 16 see other girls not doing science subjects, and they follow the majority decision, going with the herd.

Yet another reason is that a wide choice of science subjects may not be available at some schools. Recruitment of good science teachers is difficult, and certain subjects simply may not be taught. If this is the case, it is worth finding out what sixth form colleges and tertiary colleges can offer. You should certainly, long before O-levels have been taken, shop around for the most suitable A-level course in your area.

Still another reason for girls not doing science at this level is that, if they are the sole girl in a class full of boys, they may feel unwelcome and patronized. It is never easy to be the token woman, in any situation, and one can easily become discouraged by the overwhelming masculinity of a predominantly male physics class. Solidarity is always important, and it may be worth changing schools or going to a college of further education at this stage, so that you can be with other females in the class.

Women and technology

A further reason for female non-uptake of physics and chemistry may be that girls are simply not interested in science subjects as boys are. I'm not sure how far this is true, but if there is truth in the matter, it must be faced. My own impression is that girls are less interested, generally, in science applications, though they may have a similar ability as boys in coming to grips with the theory.

Not all that many girls enjoy messing about with machinery, or are very fascinated to know how the internal combustion engine works, or would be thrilled to know how they can make their own radio receiver. And there is nothing wrong with that. Interest in machines is not in itself a sign of superiority.

Computers, though, may be a different matter. We are constantly being told that we are on the brink of a computer revolution, especially in schools, and that anyone who doesn't want to be left behind like the lame boy in the Pied Piper of Hamelin story, had better bone up on computers without delay. Girls, we are informed, are in imminent danger of falling behind in the computer race, while boys are steaming ahead. A survey carried out by Acorn Computers revealed that, in households using microcomputers, boys are 13 times more likely than girls to be fiddling with the buttons. Only four per cent of mothers, it appears, regularly use micros, even when there is such a machine in the house, and even when the mother is at home all day.

Barry Newman, Computer Education Specialist for Northamptonshire Education Authority, quoted in the survey, said: 'In computers, the girls back off and the boys walk forward. The girls really have to be pushed, even if they possess a natural inclination in this direction.' Yet several schools canvassed in the survey agreed that, once the girls could be motivated, they showed themselves equally capable of coming to grips with computers.

Of course. There is nothing inherently missing in the female brain that stops a girl from learning how to use computers. One young female editor of a leading computer magazine reckoned that computer programming was about as difficult as reading a knitting pattern. And how many men can do that?

The main problem was, she felt, that girls saw microcomputers mainly as games machines and weren't particularly enthralled at the thought of zapping little green men. Though girls may be less interested than boys in computers and technology, there is no evidence to suggest that they have a lower ability. Women are actually better at logical problems, thinks Major Tom Hardy, Head of Computer Studies at Cheltenham Ladies' College. He reckons that in ten crucial areas, girls have the lead over boys.

These are: patience, an eye for detail and capacity for hard work. They are also less arrogant and self-opinionated, which makes them more willing to learn. They are closer to everyday problems and more friendly, putting themselves in the position of the user when writing programs. Added to this, girls are more methodical, respond better to discipline and are more likely to be perfectionists. And that's from a man!

There is some timidity, boredom and lack of interest among girls for computers. Ann McMullen, Director of the Electrical Institute for Women, reckons that most women are patiently waiting for computers to have some definite domestic application before they will welcome them into their hearts. 'About 60 years ago, there was the same problem with electricity,' she said. 'Women couldn't see the point of it, and that's really why our association started. We had to persuade women of the day that electricity was going to be beneficial to their lives. The same is happening now with computers. Until women see a practical application they will not tend to be all that interested.'

I can't somehow buy the idea that, in order to be a liberated woman in our society, you must be a technofreak with physics, chemistry and computer studies at A-level. But there should, certainly, be the choice to take these subjects, and girls with aptitude and interest must be encouraged, not turned away.

Science or arts?

But before deciding which A-level subjects to take, you must ask yourself whether they would be right for you. Do you honestly enjoy equations and working out rows of complicated figures? One girl, now with a first-class honours degree in maths, said: 'At A-level, I just loved going into my room and working out mathematical problems. I found it so logical, so satisfying. It was fun as well.'

That is the sort of attitude you need to have towards your A-level subjects, if you are to get the maximum from them. But if you know that a certain range of subjects is not really you, then leave them alone. There is nothing innately superior about science subjects, and definitely no point in taking a science-based course that you are never going to enjoy. There is a lingering feeling that traditional boys' subjects are somehow more important in the world at large than subjects most girls take at this stage. But if we are to become truly equal, truly liberated, we must get that sort of lumber right out of our heads. You don't have to be more intelligent to gain an A grade in physics than to acquire an A in English. It's just that the two subjects require different types of intelligence. One is not lower, or higher, than the other. English should not be regarded as a soft option, as it is a precision subject that needs maturity and vision if candidates are to do well. Poets of the past (and present) used language just as exactly as any mathematician uses figures.

There is, just now, a mighty move to attract girls into engineering jobs. At present, only seven per cent of girls are choosing to take engineering subjects at university or college. The WISE campaign – Women into Science and Engineering – organized jointly by the Equal Opportunities Commission and the Engineering Council, has sent an information pack to every secondary school in the country.

Why? Because they want women to have wonderful careers that have been denied them all these years? NO, by no means. It's mainly because they can't attract the men either that they are now focusing on the women. Looking at the whole thing dispassionately, one has to come to the conclusion that if they can't persuade men to come in, they'll have a go at the girls. Not that I'm knocking engineering as a career for girls, necessarily, but one has to be careful not to be swayed by propaganda. Whenever an expensive campaign is launched, suspicion must be aroused.

You don't see many major campaigns to attract many women into medicine, though the profession, God knows, badly needs the feminine touch. Why? Because too many women want to get in as it is. I've heard it said by several eminent women doctors that, if medical students were chosen purely on merit and academic qualifications, at least 80 per cent would be women. But there is currently a quota saying no more than 50 per cent women, please. That, if nothing else, would show that large numbers of girls are perfectly capable of getting excellent A-level results in science subjects.

Many many girls are now gaining the impression that if they want to succeed in tomorrow's world, they must become scientists and not indulge themselves with pleasant little meandering arts subjects that will get them nowhere. Science is where the jobs are, we are told.

But this is, again, propaganda that should be resisted. There is no more guarantee that a science graduate will walk straight into a good job than an arts graduate. I firmly believe there are as many career options open to arts graduates, but that these people may have to do some further training after their initial degree. In this country, we have become progressively less good at manufacturing – all the typical men's jobs of the past, in fact – and have become, instead, excellent at service industries.

This is where women can come forward. Though you may need mathematical qualifications to programme computers, you don't need any kind of science knowledge in order to *sell* them.

I have met lots of women in the computer industry, often employing hundreds of staff, but the most successful women here are selling software, rather than making programs. Heather Lamont, in her early twenties, knew nothing whatsoever about computers a couple of years ago. She is now Managing Director of Rabbit Software, a thriving British firm. All of her programmers are male, but she is the boss. So never imagine that you can't work with today's technology simply because you haven't got a science or computing background.

There are still loads of jobs that arts students can do, from public relations to personnel, to managing, to business executive positions and company directorships. An arts degree is not an automatic disqualification for entry in today's competitive world.

Attitudes and impressions
But the wrong attitudes will definitely handicap you, far more than any lack of paper qualifications. Most teenage girls want to be pretty, popular and wear nice clothes, and there is nothing wrong with this. A pretty face and smart, well-dressed appearance are always an asset, and

brighten up the world around us. But you can be all these things, and clever too. Clever girls don't have to look plain and forlorn, or be spotty and bespectacled. The image of the 'bluestocking' was no doubt conjured up by some man who wanted to stop women entering higher education. When women first began to demand degrees and further education, serious, supposedly learned, professors of medicine were saying that this urge to be educated would harm their reproductive organs. If they concentrated too much on brain work, their uteruses would suffer. This nonsense has not entirely disappeared, nor has the idea that, when jobs are scarce, they should go first to the men as this sex is most deserving. Cleverness in women need not be aligned to an offputting appearance – in fact, successful women are always the most attractive, as they exude confidence, which is the most attractive quality there is.

The most important attitude to keep in mind for eventual success is self-reliance. If you realize that you are, ultimately, alone and responsible for yourself, and that nobody else can make you happy, or guarantee you that job, then you will have overcome the first important hurdle. Romantic novels, fun though they are to read, have a lot to answer for. The paradox is that they are all written by highly successful businesswomen who are themselves earning up to £250,000 a year! Enid Blyton, who in my opinion did lasting damage to the female cause by having the butch character George (Georgina) in the Famous Five books saying: 'I'm as good as a boy any day', was herself no dependent, shrinking violet, but the hardest-working, most prolific and best-selling woman writer ever known.

Octogenarian novelist Barbara Cartland who, swathed in pink and pearls, tells us that love is all, never let any mere male stand in the way of her daily writing quota. All women who seem successful and who are in the public eye, have utilized that same quality of dedication to get them where they are. Jilly Cooper may seem fun and frothy and empty-headed but she is, in reality, a highly professional, dedicated career woman who is not easily swayed from her purpose. Neither of the women I have mentioned so far is at all 'masculine' or 'unladylike' in their personality, and they are both extremely successful.

One problem that bedevils many girls but not, on the whole, boys, is that of fervently wishing they were somebody else, or looked quite different. How many teenage girls have stood in front of the mirror, heaved a great sigh and said: oh, if only I were Chloë! If only I didn't have such a big nose/fat thighs/wear glasses, then I'd be successful. As I'm boring old me, so many girls say, I'm doomed to failure. Boys, by contrast have the attitude: how wonderful to be wonderful me! If girls could inculcate some of that self-confidence, many female problems over careers would disappear overnight.

Getting started

If you are 15 and about to decide on your O-level course, what is the best way to decide which career is the right one for you? First of all, take a sheet of paper and write down everything you can about yourself, what you like doing, what you are good at and so on. List all your hobbies and interests. Also make a list, as honestly as you can, of what you consider are your personality characteristics. Are you rather shy? Do you tend to be extrovert? Do you like meeting new people? Do you like reading? Are you good at needlework, cookery, basketball, athletics?

Then write down what you would most like to be in all the world. It can be as fantastic as you like – first woman on the moon, first doctor to discover a really effective cure for cancer, or a marvellous dancer. Make a list of the people you most admire, of either sex.

Now look at the list and you should see that it is taking some kind of shape. You will discover, through writing out your likes and dislikes, that a pattern emerges. Perhaps you love working with animals. If you are also good at science subjects, and are academic, a career as a vet might be the one for you. Remember that nothing is final at this stage, as you are just trying to give yourself an idea of what you might be suited to in later life.

When making the list, also write down any physical handicaps or abilities you may have that would affect your eventual choice of career. If you are short-sighted, or flat-footed, this may modify your choice.

Do you like the idea of wearing a uniform, or of commanding a group of people? Do you like being in charge? Or are you, rather, a solitary type of person who works best on her own?

After doing all this, try to assess how you will go about getting the job you want, and whether what you have chosen is a realistic possibility. What do you know about grants, courses, qualifications needed and so on? Can you get any financial assistance while training? Will you need to live away from home? How long does the course last? If there are no grants available, will your parents be prepared to pay for you, or will you have to save up for it yourself?

You very probably won't know all the answers to these questions, but there are ways of finding out. Your local library should have a good selection of career books, but if not will be able to order these for you. It is a good idea, at this stage, to read up about possible careers that interest you. You may find that, for some, you need a particular O-level that you had not thought of taking so, if you can, read as many career books as possible in the summer holidays before deciding finally on your O-level choices. It's wonderful how motivation can act as a spur. If you know you need a particular subject, you can suddenly become extremely good at it, at least to a certain level.

If you know of an older person already in the type of job you would like to have yourself, ask them how they got there. Suppose your local GP is a woman, and you have always wanted to be a doctor. Why not pick her brains and ask how she did it, which medical school she went to, and so on. If you feel too shy to do this yourself, you could perhaps ask your mother to ask her.

On the whole, you will find that most people who are themselves in successful careers will be only too pleased to let you know how they got where they are. If your local MP is a woman, and you fancy the idea of entering politics, ask her how she made it. You could also suggest that your school invites speakers to give talks on careers – perhaps successful old girls, or women living locally who lead interesting lives.

I do feel that here, when sorting out career possibilities, it is far better to ask women, rather than men, on how they got to their present position. If you ask a man he may well give you answers that are unsatisfying or downright inapplicable. One woman psychiatrist I interviewed told me that when she applied for a higher job, the male interviewers said: 'Why do you want to go any further? You've done very well for a woman already.' At this stage she realized she would never obtain any proper advice from a man, so in future she turned to women who were already in the position she desired to be.

I will never forget reading about the experiences of Charlotte Brontë, when she was seeking advice on how to become a published writer. She wrote to Robert Southey, then Poet Laureate. He replied that, as a woman, she would be better off not to think about writing for publication at all. 'Literature cannot be the business of a woman's life and it ought not to be,' he wrote back. 'The more she is engaged in her proper duties, the less leisure she will have for it, even as an accomplishment and recreation.' This was written in 1837 and, luckily for us, Charlotte Brontë did not take his advice to heart. But do not imagine that things have changed very greatly. Many men still feel that a woman should be properly engaged in looking after them, and seeing to their comforts, rather than wanting any rewards or success for herself. Also, a man may not be aware of the particular problems that may be facing a woman. Only other women, those who have themselves been through the career mill, will understand.

Professional associations – addresses are again obtainable from the local library – will send you details of entry qualifications, training periods, where and when to apply. So after sending off for a selection of these, you can see whether they are really the kind of thing you want to do. Never choose a career simply because it sounds glamorous, or because your best friend wants to do it. You should feel a strong yearning yourself to be in that career.

Careers advice

After reading and thinking about possible careers, you may wonder whether you are in fact suited to the ones that seem to attract you. You may be able to sort it out easily with your careers teacher, or local careers advisor. But if you remain unconvinced by what they say, you may consider going for a proper careers analysis. These are carried out by industrial psychologists, and consist of a series of aptitude tests, nothing like school examinations, which show which job would be the most suitable for you.

George Summerfield, who started Careers Analysts over 20 years ago, said: 'Our tests give clear guidance on how to set about choosing a career, with answers to questions such as: should you study for A-levels, would it be right to apply for university, and if so, which courses should be considered?

'We don't automatically recommend science and maths A-levels and university to every girl we see. If you haven't got a real interest in the subject you won't be motivated and, therefore, you are unlikely to do well. This doesn't apply to O-level, but it certainly does at higher stages of the subject. Some people may like the *idea* of being scientists, but you must first be practical.'

The aptitude tests that you would take with a careers analyst – usually at their premises to ensure fair play – are designed to find out what you are really like, and to separate what you enjoy from what you are actually good at. The tests reveal such information as whether you are good at reasoning with words, whether you are a lateral thinker, whether you are numerically gifted. The answers that come up in careers tests are often surprising.

They can also answer such dilemmas as whether you would be better off in a big organization or working with a few people. Are you a company woman or a rugged individualist? Are you a rural or a town person? Would you be happier working with people or things? The test can sort all these problems out, and avoid you becoming a square peg in a round hole.

'Girls who can do mechanical tests easily are the ones who might become engineers,' George Summerfield said. 'You would also need a high level of abstract numeracy, an ability to come to grips with a diagrammatic learning, and also the personality to cope with being a woman in a mainly man's world. The personality aspect is as important as the academic aptitude, and you have to understand the environment you are likely to be working in, before making a definite decision.

'Some girls have all the theoretical abilities to cope with an engineering job, but would be too shy and reserved to last long in a noisy factory where dirty jokes may be flying around all the time. That is why we say no girl should ever consider doing a 'man's' job simply as a protest, or out of a sense of rebellion. Some girls are ideally suited to these jobs, but you must first of all make sure.'

Very often, the right choice may be an unusual one. In her book *Equal Opportunities – A Careers Guide*, Ruth Miller mentions all kinds of non-obvious jobs, such as landscape architecture, patent agent, air traffic controller, remedial gymnast, information scientist. Most people tend to think in terms of about a dozen careers, but there are all kinds of exciting possibilities, once you start exploring the field. So many careers bear no relation at all to school subjects, and anybody who is not at all sure of what they would like to do, may consider a proper careers analysis. It will currently cost you – or your parents – around £100.

It should be realized that not everybody would be best off by staying at school or college. Some 16-year-olds would be advised to leave school and start their apprenticeship or training straight away. If you don't actually like school, and find learning a chore and a bore when it is unrelated to the practical world, you may be someone who is better off doing this.

Hairdressing, for example, is a career that may be shunned by some girls who see it as something of a dead-end job. Yet if you think about it, hairdressing has much to offer. It is creative, you meet people, and there are many opportunities to travel, set-up in business on your own, and give pleasure to people.

Is it a good idea to get some secretarial training, even when you may not want to be a secretary? It is true that those with secretarial skills need never be unemployed. It is also true that a secretarial course is often the last resort for girls who can't think what the hell to do, and feel they might as well arm themselves with some shorthand and typing, as this will never come amiss. After leaving university, I took an evening course in typing and am glad I did, as I can now touch type very quickly, which is an asset when you are a writer, although I never intended to become a secretary or a typist.

But, having said that, I know many people who, not knowing what else to do with themselves, have taken secretarial courses and have then found that doors open which might otherwise have been closed. My literary agent, Maggie Noach, left school with no clear idea of what she wanted to do, and became a secretary. She took a job with a firm of literary agents, and then found her vocation.

Many many secretaries have gone on to become formidable career women. Once in a job, they realized that being a secretary was not enough for them, and so they worked their way up to more exciting jobs. Verity Lambert, now head of Euston Films, was once a secretary, so was Felicity Green, formerly associate editor on the Daily Express.

So my advice is: try to think of some alternatives to being a secretary, but if you can't, then a secretarial course will certainly get you into an office that might not otherwise consider employing you. Being a secretary is often a way into magazine journalism, advertising, public relations, politics, publishing – in fact, all the more fluid jobs where specific qualifications are not always needed. But if you know from the outset that you want to be a journalist, advertising agent or publisher, it is better to go for these at the start, rather than by the roundabout way of becoming a secretary first.

What parents can do

There is a distinct danger, with parents of either sex, that they will try to rectify their own mistakes through their children. If you did not take O-levels but now wish fervently you had, you cannot on this basis alone persuade your daughter that she ought to. Teenagers are separate individuals, and they will have to learn to make their own mistakes. It is essential for parents, as well as adolescents to realize that there is no such thing as an unbroken record of success, whatever job you aim at. Everybody who we regard as successful has, in fact, made many mistakes along the way.

The difference between successful and unsuccessful people in this respect is that the former learn from their mistakes, and don't keep repeating them. You can, though, hope that your children won't repeat *your* mistakes.

Middle-aged women who are mothers and housewives, rather than career women, often express disappointment that their teenage daughters are not more ambitious. But you can't expect your daughter to fulfil *your* ambitions. She will have to make her own mistakes, and follow her own nose. You should never try to push a child into a career because it's the one you wish you had had.

But mothers, particularly, can make a very real contribution by offering every encouragement, and being especially careful never to instil negative thoughts such as: 'You'll never amount to anything,' or, 'Why can't you be more like your brother?' Girls, even more than boys, pick up adverse criticism and take it very much to heart. Mothers can also help by making sure their daughters are given good conditions to work and study in, and not expecting them to be more available for washing up and housework than the men in the house.

There can also be pressure on girls to find a nice boyfriend, settle down and get married before a career pattern has been established. I still hear mothers of grown-up daughters saying: 'But all mothers want to see their daughters safely married.' In an American cartoon book, one middle-aged, blue-rinse type mother says to another: 'What's wrong? Isn't your daughter a highly successful doctor?' 'Yes,' the other mother wails, 'but she isn't married!'

Unfortunately, all too many older women still like to see themselves as the bride's mother, rather than wanting to bring up a girl who will be able to stand on her own feet. I'm not saying there is anything wrong with getting married, necessarily, just that girls should not consider this their main aim in life. There are too many divorces, and marriage is by no means a secure ticket to either an income or happiness.

Also, there are too many other careers around for girls to want to think of marriage as a career in itself. It is true that patterns of behaviour tend to repeat themselves in generations, so that a successful career woman will tend to have a career-minded daughter, whereas somebody who married at sixteen and never worked outside the home thereafter, will probably have a daughter who does ditto.

But any mother who feels disappointed with the way her life has worked out – and very many women do these days – should be extremely careful not to foist her frustrations onto her daughter. Teenagers aren't very interested in the life mother wishes she'd had. Also, they have enough problems of their own, without being asked to take on mum's woes as well.

Further Reading and Information

Equal Opportunities: A Careers Guide, Ruth Miller (Penguin, 6th edition. 1981).

First Steps to a Career, Kalyani Menon (Shepheard Walwyn, 2nd edition, 1981).

Invisible Women: The Schooling Scandal, Dale Spender (Writers and Readers Publishing Co-operative, 1982).

The Female Eunuch, Germaine Greer (Granada, 1981).

Danger: Men at Work. How to Make it in a Man's World, Rosalind Miles (Futura, 1982).

2

Making Progress

One could analyse for ever the reasons why there are comparatively so few women in high-earning and influential jobs, or in positions of power and prestige. However, such agonizings, while useful to bear in mind, don't actually help women to succeed. It is important to realize at the outset that, while it may be uncommon for very many women to be in satisfying jobs, it is by no means impossible to hit the heights. You *can* succeed, and hardly any doors these days are impenetrably barred and bolted. But you have to go about your career the right way and understand from the start that, whatever elevated position is finally reached, it will be as a direct result of your own efforts and determination.

No good career ever 'just happens'. One often reads interviews with successful women who, when asked the secret of their success, put it down to 'luck', whatever that may be, or being in the right place at the right time. Such vagueness ensures their secret stays safe, because it imparts no information whatsoever. Luck has, in fact, very little to do with any form of success. Though there will be, in every person's life, occurrences that look like lucky breaks, you have to be aware and clued-up enough to take advantage of them.

Every successful person, man or woman, has had to put in a lot of hard work and effort to arrive at the top. And there is no blueprint for success – anybody at all who wants to can have a good career. But first you must want a career and then, before it is achieved, keep in mind what you want out of it. The determined thought will always precede the action.

You don't need to have come from a rich background, or possess a wonderfully academic brain, or even have been to the best schools, to embark on a proper career. But if there is one thing that all successful people have in common, it is that they do not ever let initial setbacks stop them. In fact, any failures or rejections they have along the way only serve to strengthen their resolve, and make them more determined and strong-willed than ever.

What is 'feminine'?

Some women may be worried about embarking on a single-minded career path, for fear that this will label them 'unfeminine'. It is the case that, in the past, some career women did tend to feel the need to look and behave rather like honorary men. One thinks of the composer Dame Ethel Smyth, in her mannish tweeds and cropped hair, taking no nonsense at all from men. Somehow, a butch look has become associated with women trying to make it in a man's world. But actually, those pioneering days are over, and we can now relax about appearance and behaviour. In the days when most women wore tight corsets and silken gowns, any female who wanted to carve out a career for herself felt she had to look different from that, in order to be taken at all seriously.

But in reality, femininity and masculinity have very little to do with dress alone. In the eighteenth century men wore powdered wigs and shirts frothing with lace, but they were no less masculine than today's executive in his blue pin-stripe suit.

Some women 'dress for success' in an adaptation of the professional man's workwear, and buy tailored suits and sharp shirts. Others wear low-cut necklines and four-inch heels. But one is not necessarily more 'feminine' than the other.

These days, you can't tell much about a woman's femininity from her appearance. Very many non-career women, those who are content to be housewives and mothers, always wear jeans, never have a scrap of make-up on, and keep their hair in a short, utilitarian cut. By contrast, lots of extremely high-flying career women have cascades of golden hair, are always made up as if to star in a film, and wear a different eye-catching outfit every day.

Which of the two would you say was more feminine? Well, that all depends on how you define femininity. Whenever you ask a man at the top why there are so few women in his elevated position, he will reply that his high office is hardly the place for a woman. Or, trying to be funny, they will say: 'Well, we have got Miss Brown – and she's the best man in the organization.' In fact, Mrs Thatcher has very often been called 'the best man in the government', by people who are trying to pay her a compliment.

But are career women really unfeminine on the inside, whatever their outward appearance may be? If you regard a 'feminine' woman as passive, wheedling and dependent, then, yes, you do have to be unfeminine to succeed in a career. Those qualities will get you nowhere at all. But you do not have to automatically become rough, rude, aggressive, egotistical, boorish, angry and insensitive to succeed in the world outside. There is no need at all to bring the worst of the masculine qualities to a profession but rather, enhance it by displaying the best of the feminine qualities which are: tolerance, forgiveness, and slowness to anger.

You must lose the negative side of femininity, but not the positive side. I certainly don't think that having a career makes a woman more like a man, except in this: that she has learned to take responsibilty for herself, and to become self-reliant.

A positive approach

The first step on the road to a good career is not to see any work you do, however humble it may seem, as 'just a job'. This little word 'just' is one that hampers and handicaps women. How many women do you meet who inform you that they are 'just' a housewife, or 'just' a secretary, or 'just' the office dogsbody, or that they 'just' have a part-time job?

That word in itself has the power to put you down as not being worth serious consideration on the job market. In effect you are saying: 'I'm not much of a person, and not of much importance, so you needn't take any notice of me.' There is a valuable lesson here to be learned from the man's approach, as 'just' is a word you hardly ever hear them use to describe their jobs. A man will never tell you he is 'just' a carpenter, a garage hand, or lorry driver. Instead, he will want to convey the impression that he has chosen his job above all others, and there is nothing he would rather do. So, a carpenter becomes a self-employed craftsman, a garage hand becomes a motor engineer, a lorry driver a haulage contractor. So many men heading their own small business style themselves 'chairman and managing director'. Often, their letterheads will indicate a number of directors. Closer inspection reveals that these 'directors' are all their own children, parents, or aunts and uncles, put there to look good on the notepaper.

I'm not saying that we want to ape the male approach in every way, but we can learn from the positive aspects. Never undersell yourself, or present yourself in a bad light. These are the first laws of good job-getting. It won't do any harm to adopt some of the male strategies in describing your job, or even your abilities. One American researcher once did some work in schools, defining the different attitudes of boys and girls in relation to their work. Whereas a girl would tend to say: 'I only got a B plus for my last essay,' a boy's reaction would be: 'Imagine, I got a B plus last time.'

The same mark – but what a difference of attitude, and it's one that tends to bug women all their lives. Men tend to play up their achievements, whereas women play theirs down. Women tend to concentrate on their faults, whereas men will only ever point out their good qualities. We can't, at a stroke, wipe out the conditioning of centuries, but if we realize that women are liable to diminish their own achievements, we can be on our guard for signs of this behaviour. Women have also, in the past, been handicapped by their attitude towards their jobs. They have tended to be apologetic about any paid work they do, and give the impression that money-earning is in no way central to their lives and happiness.

We really will never get anywhere until this attitude is overcome, whatever legislation might be brought in. You can legislate for equal opportunities, but you can never order people to *feel* equal, or to take up the opportunities when they arise.

At the very outset, you must set yourself goals. This is of prime importance, otherwise you drift on, not knowing where you are supposed to be going. Psychologist Tom Crabtree, who writes in *Cosmopolitan* magazine, has this valuable advice on goal setting: First of all, he says, the goals must be realistic. It's no use saying: I want to be rich and famous. You have to know *how* you are going to achieve this and, more importantly, *why* you want to be rich and famous.

If setting goals is a new concept for you, here are Tom Crabtree's tips:

1. First of all, forget the past. Instead of trying to be somebody else, start being yourself.
2. Make a list of the goals you would like to achieve, and set about achieving them.
3. Don't make promises to yourself that you don't intend to keep.
4. Concentrate on your own goal. There will be plenty of people who try to persuade you to help them reach *their* goals. (It's very common for a wife to help her husband get to the top, be a good hostess for him, make a nice home and so on, but rare, so rare, the other way round.)
5. Don't compare goals – just get there. Let others climb Everest, and you choose your own hills to climb.
6. Start with reachable goals, then work hard towards more ambitious ones.

You may, for some reason, have missed out on an academic school career, and left school at 15 or 16. Perhaps you hated school, hated work, or hated your teachers. It is a fact that girls do less well in subjects when they dislike the teacher, and tend to shine in those subjects where the teacher is popular. Anyway, for whatever reason, you have left school without that clutch of O- and A-levels that would seem to open up career doors. Is all lost? Not a bit of it. You can still set yourself goals and, one by one, begin to achieve them.

It is true that nobody will give you a good job, just like that, when you are very young, have no experience of the working world, and have few paper qualifications to offer either. But you can still see the eventual job you do get as an important step along the way. I feel it is far better to get a job – any job – than going straight onto the dole and getting out of bed at noon each day. That way of life rapidly leads to depression which, in turn, can lead to anger and frustration. There is *no need at all* for anybody to be unemployed. There is always something you can do, from taking next door's dog for a walk, to getting on with your novel, to typing out people's theses. There can never be any excuse at all for sitting around all day doing nothing.

For most school leavers, however, the first hurdle to overcome is to land that very first job. These days it can take some doing but, with the right attitude, you can do it. Whenever you go for a job you are liable to find yourself in competition with many other young people, and it can be very easy to lose heart and feel you are rejected before you even start. You must never – ever – give up, though, and, however hopeless it seems, continue to write letters, apply for jobs and seek out opportunities.

First impressions: the curriculum vitae

When looking for a job, your initial aim is to make a good impression. If you can't write letters very well, ask somebody who can to help you, whether this is a teacher at school, your parents or a youth leader. Beg a competent typist to type out a curriculum vitae for you. This is simply a record of yourself, with job experience, schooling and any qualifications listed as briefly as possible. In a CV, always be honest while, at the same time, giving the best possible impression of yourself. Don't say you can drive if you can't, or put down any O-levels you have taken but failed. If you have failed exams, just don't mention them.

When preparing a CV, always start with now, working backwards in time. Begin with your latest job, giving months or years worked and the exact position you held – it can always be checked up – and then give a brief history of your school career, mentioning any hobbies or positions of responsibility. If you have a Duke of Edinburgh Award, or a gold medal for swimming, put these down, even if they seem to have no direct relevance to your job. These factors always give potential employers information about your character and suitability for the position, and can show perseverance and the ability to achieve something.

So this is the order: jobs, with dates; school career, with dates; schools attended and exams passed; other relevant information. After preparing your CV, have a dozen or so copies made at a print shop or your local library. Potential employers know that you are likely to be sending round a CV to several firms, so won't mind seeing a photocopy. *Don't*, though, whatever you do, ever photocopy letters of application for jobs. These must always be individually written to a human being, rather than addressing the boss as 'Dear Sir'. If you don't know exactly who to apply to, it is quite in order to ring up the firm and find out, also checking on how the name is spelt. Even simple-sounding names can be spelt in an odd way. I once applied for a job to a 'Mr Collins' and back came a reply from a 'Mr Colyns', which just shows you can never be too careful. Attention to detail such as this all adds up to seriousness and determination, which can make a lot of difference when you are applying for first jobs, and trying to get started.

After preparing your CV, you should ask at least two people, whom you know well, to give you a reference. Ideally, these should be people in positions of some authority or consequence, such as a doctor, solicitor, head teacher or bank manager. It is always a good idea, whenever you leave a particular job, to ask your former employer to write you out a reference. When jobs are hard to get, these strategies all help.

What shall I do?
But all this is of little use unless you have some idea of the kind of jobs you would like to apply for. If you are steaming ahead on your way to becoming a doctor, journalist or barrister, this section of the book may not apply to you. But even if you are safely at college or university, it helps to have some idea of the goals you may be aiming at. If you are studying law, ask yourself: do I want to be a barrister or solicitor, and why? Is it the pay, the hours, the prestige, the chance to help people, the opportunity to bring a much-needed womanly approach to the profession? Where would I see myself in five years' time?

If training to be a doctor, constantly monitor your progress, asking yourself whether you want to be a GP or a hospital doctor, work with children or be a surgeon. It is better to aim at some branch of the profession that will genuinely suit you, rather than to go for a job that will fit in nicely with being a wife and mother. This approach can put the blinkers on a career long before you ever start.

There is plenty of time to worry about all that sort of thing later. After all, you can have babies when in your early forties, but you may not get another chance to train for a good career. Put first things first, if you have made up your mind that you want a proper career. (And if you don't – what are you doing reading this book?)

Today, girls are often encouraged to go in for science training, as they are told that this is where all the good jobs are. This may be so, but there is little point in struggling to obtain qualifications and applying for jobs when your heart is not in what you are doing. Of course, there should be every opportunity to take up scientific subjects for girls who enjoy these and are good at them. But if you don't like the idea of being employed in an engineering works, don't, for goodness sake, take qualifications which will put you there. The whole idea of having a good job is that it enhances your life in a way no other activity can. If you don't enjoy your work at all, you will never do it well, and are likely to spend your time at your job feeling miserable and resentful. In time, this will inevitably affect your performance at work.

To go back to the girl who hasn't any idea what she would like to do, doesn't want to embark on further study, but would like a good job doing *something*. What should she do? Is her position hopeless? No, but it may take longer to sort out exactly the right career path. If you recognize yourself as this sort of girl, ask yourself what in life interests you most. Do you like fashion and are you excited by new clothes? Then why not apply for a job in a department store? They are almost always short of staff. If, once you are there, you like the life, you can then ask about training schemes for managerial posts, or becoming a buyer. Many large stores, such as Littlewoods, John Lewis, and the House of Fraser have training schemes, and are only too willing to encourage ambitious girls.

Andrée Grenfell took a holiday job in a West End store at fifteen, and decided she liked the life so much that she never returned to school to take her A-levels. Instead, she trained as a manager, and by the age of thirty had become a director of Peter Robinson. She went on to an even more glittering career in the retail, and, later, beauty trade. The upward path can indeed be rapid, once you have set your sights. But nothing will ever happen unless you have a clear end in view.

You may discover, on obtaining a job in a shop or store, that you don't like it at all. You may not enjoy the constant standing, having to be polite, or the lack of fresh air. In that case, you have still learned a valuable lesson, and are that much nearer to deciding what you *would* like to do. You have overcome the first hurdle, and can now cross off a whole list of indoor jobs that you would not enjoy. But, before leaving anywhere in disgust, think out carefully what you would prefer to do instead. Work with animals, perhaps? One school friend of mine, with little interest in, or aptitude for academic pursuits, left school at fifteen to work in a famous fashion shop. After two years there, she decided she was pining for the outdoor life. She had always been passionately fond of dogs, and wondered about working with them, in some capacity. After taking a job in kennels to tide her over, she began to breed dogs herself, and is now a highly successful breeder of unusual miniature canines. But like everybody else, she had to start somewhere.

A job will always open up horizons, however minor that job may be. A girl who is not academic, but who wants to get away from home, can quite easily find herself a job as a mother's help. You don't even have to have been to a nursery training college to do this work. Many, many career women are now on the lookout for responsibly-minded girls to look after their children and help round the house. You must actually like children, of course, otherwise this job could be unbearable.

Though such a job may not seem very high powered, it can lead on to other things. You may become fired by enthusiasm for what your employer is doing, and decide to emulate her. At the very least you will be feeding additional input into your life, and getting in a better position to discover what you really want to do. One former nanny, Sheila Bell, decided after working in London that there could be distinct possibilities in starting an agency that would put girls from the North in touch with London employers. She now runs Northumberland Nannies. So never dismiss a job opportunity because it sounds mundane or servile. The only servility comes in the attitude with which you work. There is nothing in itself low or mean about looking after other people's children and, for some girls, it can provide an ideal breather between school and launching oneself into a full-time, non-stop career.

Whenever you don't know what to do, look for possibilities, rather than mooching around, and expecting somebody to ring you up out of the blue and offer you a fantastic job. Perhaps you have tried and tried, and still nobody offers you even a glimmer of a job. You can always clean people's houses, weed flower beds, or babysit. You can wash cars. A good way to do this is to have some leaflets printed detailing the services you offer – costs next to nothing if you type them out and then have, say, 1,000 run off – and deliver them to people's doors. Choose your area carefully – there's not much point in offering gardening services where there are only high rise flats, or where most people are out of work.

You never know when you may come across just that right person who will get you started on the job you really want. But eternal vigilance is essential. Even a paper round should not be despised, though the work may be boring and badly paid. There are so many free papers about now, and they all need putting in people's letterboxes.

Danger areas

Whatever you achieve in life, it will come about directly as a result of your own efforts. No effort leads to no results. Nobody should ever expect that somebody else will magically come to lift them out of their rut and transport them into some wonderful job that pays well, has short hours and doesn't involve any aggro. Far too many women do still, unfortunately, have the longing for somebody to take them away from all this. It's a deep-rooted feeling that is explored at length in Colette Dowling's book *The Cinderella Complex: Women's Hidden Fear of Independence*. Women do still tend to fear independence, or to be ready to give up their work for some man. How many middle-aged women today do you hear saying that they gave up a promising career so that their husbands could get on? A career can always be 'promising' so long as it is never put to the test. But any woman who truly wants to be independent will have to make a commitment to herself always to be able to stand on her feet, and not to expect anybody else to come along to take the burden off her shoulders.

In the previous chapter, we spoke about going to secretarial college, and asked whether this was a trap for the career-bound woman. If you do learn to type, does this condemn you to being a typist for ever more? Though there is nothing wrong at all in obtaining secretarial qualifications to add to your armoury of job-market skills, it is important to realize that secretaries are not, usually, thought of as career women. So, if you have any thoughts about doing something specific, stay away from the secretarial jobs. They are a trap, in my view, and they do limit and confine you. It is less easy than it used to be to use shorthand and typing as stepping stones to a more individual career but again, it is better to be a secretary than not to have a job at all.

There is yet another trap for the unwary secretary that can very much affect a woman's working life: she may fall in love with her boss. The teacher-pupil, master-servant relationship, beloved of so many romantic novels, is still potent for so many girls. It is very often not so much the boss himself that she falls in love with, as his position. While women put themselves into subordinate-type jobs, this remains a very real danger. There is still, unfortunately, status in going out with one's employer – or, at least, there is when women have a passive, dependent attitude towards themselves. Office romances usually end in tears, for the girl, or dismissal or demotion. The boss himself is almost always considered too important to be removed, though he will very often be the one who instigates the affair.

Rosalind Miles argues in her book *Danger – Men at Work*, that office romances are all a plot to keep women down and in their place. But it takes two, and office affairs cannot flourish without some compliance on the part of the woman concerned. One can't help noticing, though, that a man in an executive position rarely embarks on an affair with a woman who is his professional equal. It is almost always someone lower down the line.

While you are engaged in a love affair especially if it is conducted clandestinely, your mind cannot be wholly concentrated on your work. Career women do fall in love in the same way as other women, but they should not yearn for it all the time, nor want to be admired for their ability to make men go weak at the knees. That is not the sort of power that the working woman should aim at. All serious career women should want to be admired for the excellence of their work, which isn't to say you can't be light and humorous and good company. Your company can still be very enjoyable, and you can enhance any gathering, without making eyes at the managing director.

First impressions: persistence and appearance
For most people, the hardest job of all to land is the first one, and this applies whether you are a 16-year-old school leaver or a graduate with a string of honours degrees behind you. Whatever your age and stage, when you apply for that first job, you have no professional experience behind you and this will inevitably count in your disfavour. If you don't believe me, look at a few job ads in the papers, and you will see that they almost always require some relevant experience. Getting started is the problem, always, and it is even more of a problem for a woman than a man.

As the potential job market may be more confusing to the teenager, I'll address this section of would-be employees first. I said earlier that you must prepare a CV and also, be prepared to take any job rather than do nothing. But what if you know exactly what you would like to do? First of all, the time to start applying for jobs is not in July, when you will have left school or college, but January. Think hard about the types of job that you could do now, without extra training and whether you would be prepared to do a year or more of further training. If the job you want is a long way from home, does it pay enough to enable you to live in a flat or lodgings?

Write in reply to all the vaguely suitable ads you see and keep looking for job openings. If nothing suitable seems to be advertised, write to the people who might possibly give you employment. Be prepared here for outright rejections, refusals, and permanent silences. Anne Diamond, the breakfast TV presenter, said recently that she once applied for jobs on 47 different newspapers, and only one even bothered to reply. But on average, you can expect to receive a reply for every ten jobs for which you apply, and a job for every ten interviews you attend. Many, many employers are receiving just such applications as yours, and have not the time or inclination to acknowledge them all.

Write politely but confidently, stating that you would like the chance to get started, and would be grateful for any advice or information, should an actual job not be available at present. If you don't hear, after six weeks or so, follow up your initial letter and ask again. Remind them of your existence, without being rude, cringing or self-pitying, and repeat your request for information. Thirdly, you could telephone the firm, reminding them that you are the girl who wrote, and that you are very keen indeed to get a job in that particular line. Ask if it might be possible to come and see the manager, even though there may not be a job at present.

People who are blessed with this kind of persistence seldom remain unemployed for long. Everybody is impressed with courage, determination and guts, and these qualities, in the end, count far more than impressive exam results. After all, you are hardly likely to need an O-level in Latin on the job, unless you become an archivist or Latin teacher, but you will certainly require large amounts of determination, if you are to get anywhere at all.

A note on voice and dress: I keep meeting middle-aged people who voice surprise that a youngster with such and such a haircut, or wearing a certain type of outfit should ever expect to get a job at all. 'I wouldn't employ her,' they say. Teenagers can be very arrogant about their dress and take the attitude: if they don't like me as I am, they can stuff their job. But arrogance over dress often hides a great insecurity. Outrageous dress has two main functions: it serves to shock the mouldy oldies, and it makes you a member of that exclusive teenage club: the cool dresser. Really way-out dress will always limit your chances – very few companies want a budding pop star in their employment – but voice and manner will limit you even more.

My advice to job-seeking girls is: do look fashionable rather than boring, but tone down the outer limits. Posture and bearing will work wonders, and a girl who stands up straight, has a ready smile and never looks sullen immediately puts herself in the front of the job queue. Teenagers often do slouch and have a sullen appearance, thinking this makes them look more mature and knowledgeable than they really are. But it just has the opposite impression on the average employer.

Myself, I don't so much mind about clothes, and would have no objection to employing someone with green hair, or a ring through their nose. I think teenage experimentation is fun, and so much better than having everybody looking dull and boring in grey suits. But I am prejudiced over voices, and wouldn't want to employ a girl with a horrible voice, particularly if the job involved telephoning clients. Unfortunately, a certain 'twang' has become very common among young people. If only they could realize that those with pleasant voices, who were well-spoken and articulate, could almost walk straight into a job, I'm sure those awful, lazy voices would disappear.

Mrs Thatcher learned early the importance of a good voice, as did newsreader Sue Lawley. Both came from very lower-middle class backgrounds, but made a conscious decision to learn to talk properly – and look where it got them. They had other qualities as well, of course, but the voice was all part of the paying attention to detail that marks a person out for success.

It is the highest common factor that should be aimed at, rather than the lowest common denominator. If you have an attractive voice, people immediately think that you are somebody. These days, the voice is more important than ever before.

As a journalist, I often get to know really well people I have never met, because I talk to them a lot on the phone. As the phone is all I have to go on, their voice has to be their ambassador. And so it is for an increasing range of jobs these days. You do not have to want to be on radio or television to be judged very much on a good speaking voice. In today's world, the spoken voice is more important than at any other time in history, as so much communication is made via the telephone. Good handwriting used to be one way to a good job but now, with typewriters and word processors, a good hand counts for less and less. It is the case that big companies do often retain handwriting experts, but this is usually only to assess top-level employees. Nice handwriting would not get you noticed these days, as job applications must always be typewritten, unless the job ad specifically states otherwise.

If you know your voice is holding you back, why not invest in private speech lessons? Almost all local colleges run these and they have very little to do with old-fashioned elocution.

When you have few paper qualifications, and are very young and inexperienced, you must make the very most of the assets you do have. It is all right for someone such as Janet Street-Porter to speak on television with her exaggerated Cockney accent but she talks with great confidence, and her voice has become an integral part of her trade mark. This overrides the grating, irritating effect of this type of voice, as it is almost a comedy act in itself. But anybody who is anxious to get started would do well not to imitate her. You do not have to lose a regional accent and speak BBC English, but your speech must be clear and grammatical.

Whole books have been written on interview techniques, and you do not need to mug up on them all. A few essentials to remember are: always be on time, even early. You should allow at least half an hour to spare if catching a train or bus, to replace your tights, if necessary, go to the loo, do your hair or adjust your make-up. If the time set by the firm for your interview is not convenient, and you just can't make it, say so at once, and ask for an earlier or later time. Don't just meekly say 'yes', knowing that there is no suitable public transport at that hour, or you won't be able to leave your present job at that time.

Also, before actually going for the interview, find out as much as you can about the firm that might be taking you on, and exactly what your job is likely to entail. Everybody is nervous at interviews, even the interviewer, so, before going in, practise a few deep breathing exercises. These really do help, as they slow down your heartbeat, and stop it from racing and thumping against your chest.

Next, do have some answers to questions ready, as to why you would like the job, and why you think you would be the ideal person to fill the position, as you are sure to be asked.

When you are actually sitting in front of the interviewer, try always to look him or her in the eye, without staring hypnotically. This gives an impression of calm self-assurance, and makes you seem honest and reliable. Very many young people have great difficulty in looking at others straight in the eye, so before going for the interview, practice with a friend. It may seem a small thing, but it will work wonders.

Remember that you will always appear less nervous to others than you feel to yourself. Never, ever, smoke when going for job interviews, and refuse any cigarettes that may be offered. You can always make up for it outside, if you have to!

Do not, either, have a glass of wine or beer beforehand to steady your nerves. Any alcohol may go straight to your head and make you feel woozy, and less than fully alert.

If, after the interview, you hear that you have not landed the job, it is quite in order to write to the firm, thanking them for seeing you, and saying that you would still be interested in a job with them, should another suitable vacancy arise. This helps to lodge you more firmly in their minds, and stop them forgetting all about you.

When applying for jobs and going for interviews, remember the old adage: more flies are caught by honey than vinegar. Remain polite, even when you feel you have been rejected unfairly. Unfortunately, things are far from fair in the jobs world, and expecting them to be could make you miserable. Being angry takes up time and effort, yet achieves precisely nothing. In fact, it achieves less than nothing, as it saps energy.

Actual unfair dismissal is another matter, which will be dealt with in a later chapter.

After university

Those who are gifted academically can put off the search for a job until much later, until paper qualifications are coming out of their ears. But here, as well, it helps to have some sort of goal in mind, and to understand why you are so anxious to have so very many letters after your name. Unless you have ambitions in the academic world, or know that a further degree would help to further your career, there is not much mileage in taking an MA or MPhil after your first degree. Don't take degree after degree out of a sense of frustration and failure. This is the 'if in doubt, go to college' idea, which may be a way of staving off the evil day when you will have to confront yourself with your job chances. I hear that in India the current fashion is for middle class girls to take several degrees, and put off for even longer getting an actual job.

If you really want to write a book about Shelley's feminism, or the definitive treatise on quantum physics, then a PhD might just give you the time, space and research facilities that would be impossible to obtain in any other way. But you must feel positive about it, not take more degrees because you can't be bothered to look for a job. The day of reckoning always arrives at some stage.

Graduates can be under the impression that they are extra-employable because of their superior education – and then find themselves in for a considerable shock. It is not that easy to get a job after leaving university, unless your degree course was very specifically vocational. The outside world will not, at the outset at least, be clamouring for your services, and it will be up to you to persuade them that you will fit the bill. The well-known 'milk round' exists mainly to find people for jobs that may be hard to fill, such as in retail management or certain forms of industry. If you want one of the so-called 'glamorous' jobs, for example in advertising, public relations, journalism or broadcasting, then you must be prepared for a lot of hard work and a lot of rejections.

I personally never found university careers departments of the slightest use whatsoever, but they may have improved since my day. They then seemed to want to send all women into teaching. As a very recent graduate you may not, on the face of it, have very much more to offer than any other very recent graduate, which is why extra persistence is necessary. But, and I can't say this too strongly – never be put off because the job you want may be hard to break into at the early stages. As with all assault courses, the weaker sisters soon drop out, and only the brave and determined continue the fight. Here is an example of how to get a job in a highly competitive profession. Jill was reading history at Oxford, and soon realized she wanted to be a journalist. Knowing that she could find it hard, she offered her services to women's magazines during the holidays, as a general dogsbody – opening envelopes, making tea, running errands, for practically no pay. After she graduated, she applied for an actual staff job with a national magazine – and got it – *because they already knew her*. Another girl, similarly desperate to break into journalism, offered to work for a local newspaper for nothing, when all her job applications fell on blind eyes. She worked two days a week for nothing and, for income, took a part-time job in a bookshop. It wasn't long before she, too, was in national journalism.

The secret of early success is, apply and apply and apply – and you will very soon land a job. It may not be the job of your dreams, but it will be a step on the way.

Making a change

Right. Through persistence, talent or whatever, you landed that job, but now it is no longer satisfying to you. It has ceased to become a challenge, and you now feel you are in a rut. Or perhaps you got the job you are now in when you didn't feel very ambitious, and you now feel capable of something better. Or, yet again, perhaps you have been in the same job for a number of years, and would now like to try something different.

Where do you go from here? First, you must ask yourself exactly what it is you no longer like about your present job. Is it the pay, the hours, the lack of responsibility? Don't you like the boss, the set-up, the office or the location? Working out exactly where your dissatisfaction lies will help you to make a sensible choice next time round.

It is never a good idea to leave one job purely out of pique, or simply because you feel underpaid and undervalued. You will be underpaid and undervalued in your next job as well, unless you take steps to prevent it. You actually teach people how they should regard you, and you are the only one who can remove a chip on your shoulder.

If you feel in a definite rut, and that there are few promotion possibilities in your present position, you should start looking round for something else rather than hoping things will improve where you are. But at this stage, tell nobody that you are looking. All offices have their members of staff who are always on the point of leaving, yet 20 years later are to be found in exactly the same position. Do not ever grumble, as it makes you seem impotent, but resolve to alter any situation that has become untenable. A rut, though, is a personal matter. What some people may consider to be a rut-like job, to others is very nice and cosy.

Never let other people's views influence your outlook on your job.

But before starting to look round, ask yourself these vital questions: why am I in this rut? Is it the job itself, or is it something to do with me? If I move on, will it be simply to another rut in another office? What would I prefer to do? Would a better job require further training? Do I like the size and feel of my present office, or would I like one smaller or larger? Do I like working with a lot of people, or with a few, or on my own? If the job I would like to go onto needs more training, how would I set about getting that training? Are there grants available? Can it be done on day-release, or at evening classes?

You should also ask yourself what sort of salary you eventually hope to obtain, and how important a particular pay level is to you. Once you have faced these questions, you are ready to do something about your new job. Here is a personal example. After university, I got a job as a teacher in a local girls' grammar school. I hadn't been in it very long before I realized that teaching was not the job for me. Help! What was I to do? Here I was, in a relatively well-paid and secure job, and I hated it. Should I leave it quickly, or get something else lined up first?

I knew that, all along, I had wanted to be a writer but, foolishly, did not pursue this aim enough to get myself a suitable job before graduating. I had allowed myself to be put off by people telling me journalism was too competitive, that I didn't stand a chance, and that the profession was hopelessly overcrowded anyway.

But, as teaching would never do for me, I set about applying to all the local papers in the area where I was living. None of them were in the slightest bit interested in me. Eventually, I sat down and wrote an article and sent it off to my local evening paper. The editor didn't publish it, but said he would be interested to see other efforts. The next article I wrote actually was published, and it led to a fortnightly slot, which in turn became a weekly slot. Not a very big deal, perhaps, but it got me started in journalism. I sweated blood over these articles, for which I was paid £5 a time. But they got me out of teaching, and into something which was very much more congenial to me.

One giveaway sign of being in a job you hate is that you always want to take time off, to start late and leave early. There should never be that Monday morning feeling, if you are in the job that is truly right for you.

There is, I believe, a job that is right for everybody. Journalism was me, and it has been 'me' for the past 15 years. Others know that acting is what they must do, though they may not fully realize this at first. One friend decided, at the age of 30, that she wanted to be an actress. She had trained as a biologist, and wondered at first whether she was doing the right thing. But she got into acting school, and soon landed herself some jobs. She hasn't found life all that easy, professionally speaking, since throwing up her 'safe' job, but she is doing what she wants to do.

Another friend decided, rather late in life, that she wanted to be a doctor. She had three children, was over 30, and didn't even have the relevant A-levels. Her feeling at first was: in six years' time when I have qualified, I shall be 40. Then she thought: in six years' time I shall be 40 anyway, so why not train now? She has now nearly finished her course.

Another woman, working in a factory, decided that she really hated her job. She hadn't much education and was not honestly up to passing even O-levels. So a college course was out of the question. Her problem was solved when she took a job which involved going round offices cleaning telephones. Not all that high powered, perhaps, and hardly better paid than her factory job, but how much more enjoyable. She loves her new job, which takes her out and about, and she is always meeting new people.

You don't need a string of degrees to secure the job that suits you best, but you do need the strength of purpose to land it for yourself. Nobody else can put the ambition there for you. Some older women feel they have missed out by not having somebody who would encourage them. This may be true, and regrettable, but you can never order anyone else to give you encouragement. Florence Nightingale had the very opposite of encouragement from her family, who were horrified when she announced she was going to train as a nurse, but she did it just the same.

Nobody can do your job-searching for you. The advice usually given to poets is: look into your heart and write. Exactly the same could apply to jobs. Look into your heart, and ask yourself what you truly want to do.

Many women, and men too, for that matter, have a mistaken idea of security when it comes to a job. They will tend to take a job that seems safe, even if it's not too exciting. But being in an unstimulating job for years on end really is a rotten way to spend your life. The only real security is that which comes from inside yourself, and all the pension schemes, redundancy guarantees and contracts in the world will not make you feel inwardly secure. That comes from innate self-confidence, which in turn comes from setting and attaining goals in life.

Self-confidence grows the more you are able to take risks, and put your fate into your own hands. All those who we regard as successful have, at some time in their lives, decided to shape their own destinies, and back a hunch. In other words, they believed in themselves. In order to become anything at all, you must first imagine yourself in that role. Then the thought will eventually take you there, but without the thought in the first place you can never hope for a good career.

Nobody ever saw a little secretary sitting in the corner, conscientiously erasing a rare mistake and said: 'Miss Smith, you're too good for this kind of work. I'm going to make you managing director.' At which point Miss Smith reveals herself as really dynamic, able in an instant to make the sales graph rise and rise. That may be the stuff that films were once made of, but unfortunately it is not rooted in reality. Similarly, I don't believe anyone gets anywhere by sleeping with the boss. And even if they do, it is a dastardly way of 'getting on'. Today's woman should have no need of the casting couch, which leads only to unhappiness and bitterness in the end.

Sexual harassment

Something we have been hearing a lot about lately is sexual harassment at work. Is this a real problem, or something made up by the media? And how central is it to the ambitious career woman? Rosalind Miles devotes a lot of space to this question in her book, and feels it is all-pervasive, subtle, and must be recognized and put firmly in its place.

According to surveys carried out both here and in America, there is hardly a woman working in a mixed office who has not had to put up with some form of harassment from the opposite sex. Sexual harassment came home to me in a dramatic way when I worked in a large national newspaper office. One senior member of staff asked me out and, though I instantly refused, I felt quite flattered to be asked. On mentioning this to a female colleague, I discovered he had done exactly the same to her. I soon found out that this gentleman had propositioned almost every female in the office in just the same way. What a let down. In my case there was no harm done, as it happened, but I quickly learned a valuable lesson.

It became clear to me that sexual harassment is simply something men do to women, most often in the hearing of other males, and it is especially noticeable in the office context. It usually takes the form of risqué remarks or questions, couched in the guise of a joke or a tease.

One problem is that, because women have so often been taught to defer to men and because also, the male doing the harassing will very often be in a superior position in the office hierarchy, this kind of behaviour can be very difficult indeed to combat. In fact, whole books have been written giving advice on how to deal with sexual harassment in the office.

Sometimes aggressive strategies are advised. In answer to an invitation to a dirty weekend, you could go up to the man in all seriousness and say: You know that dirty weekend you mentioned? What about the weekend after next?

My own feeling is that most women would be too shy and timid to attack like this, and that quite different tactics would probably be more likely to succeed. If you return aggression with aggression, it keeps the game going and can breed antagonism. And women must take at least some of the blame for sexual harassment. In our society, we keep being told that we should look 'sexy', which gives men some grounds, at least they feel, for the remarks they make. I'm not suggesting that correct office wear should be a nun-like shroud, but you can do a lot to help yourself in the first instance if you make no attempt to look or act in an overtly sexy manner. It is perfectly possible to look attractive without sending out sexual messages to your male workmates.

I'm sure the best way to respond to verbal harassment is simply not to hear it. Just smile politely and take no notice of what is being said. Harassing is rather like teasing – you can only ever tease the teasable, and it is hard to keep the remarks flying when they fall on deaf ears. In reality, men in offices are as insecure and nervous as the women probably are, and they take refuge in bullying tactics and bluster. If you can just simply stay serene when such remarks are made, they will just vanish like morning dew.

Promotion

Now for the vexing subject of promotion. It has been found, in countless managerial surveys, that while bright young men are quickly noticed and promoted accordingly, bright young women often mysteriously stay where they are. It is most common for recent graduates to be appointed to a technical-type job. Ten years later almost all the male graduates will be firmly on the managerial ladder, while a disproportionate amount of the female graduates will be stuck in their technical jobs.

Every large company encounters this problem, that the men steam ahead while the women tend to stay put. There used to be the attitude on the part of men that there was little point in promoting a woman because, as soon as she got to the good job, she would turn round and have a baby, leaving never to return.

Men are not allowed to say this now, and certainly not allowed to give possible pregnancy as a reason for non-promotion. But nobody can stop them *thinking* that women are liable to leave, and this affects their promotion decisions.

There is little logic in this attitude, which unfortunately remains prevalent. It is the case that any ambitious young male executive on the climb would be unlikely to stay in the same job for more than a couple of years. In the early years of their careers, at least, they would be constantly on the move, and would not give more service than a woman who left after a couple of years to have a baby.

No, marriage and possible motherhood are not the reasons why women are not promoted, though this is still most often the reason given. The real answer is that any large, middling, or even small-sized company operates very much like a man's club, with the all-male values coming to the fore. Men learn early in life that rigid hierarchical structures form the very basis of our present society, in schools, offices, and in the professions. Women, somehow, don't see these rules, are unaware of them, or ignore them. They are far less likely to form themselves into teams, or to want to work for the corporate good.

Thus, an all-woman outfit will tend to see itself as a 'collective', where all workers are equal, whereas an all-male office is usually highly autocratic, with men lower down the ladder deferring to those at the top. I remember once being told, by a bright young middle-management executive that, in order to arrive at the top, you must actually *think* like your boss, even to the extent of taking the same daily newspapers. It is hard for a woman to see the importance of this kind of behaviour, which sounds distinctly creepy. The young man who gave me this advice did go on to rise very dramatically in his company, so he must have known what he was talking about.

Men at the bottom don't mind deferring to those at the top, because they see themselves in that very position one day. The whole idea of fagging at public schools was so that little boys could learn to be servants in order to know how to become masters.

Those who are avid for promotion in a man's world will have to come to terms with this structure, and accept it for what it is. It doesn't mean that it is completely impossible for a woman to be promoted, but she must first understand, and get to know the game that these men are playing. Men learn to conform. A young female executive finds it difficult because, very often, she simply won't think like a man.

Men play work games by the rules, which they have invented, and this is mainly why they win promotion. Women are left behind, not because they are less bright or less capable, but because they are more maverick. Male bosses feel that women are unpredictable. They try to put it down to women being more emotional, and constantly liable to suffer from premenstrual tension, whereas in fact, there is nobody more emotional than a man. Women are called 'emotional' because they tend to do things a man would never do.

Women executives are, if anything, far less emotional than men. But male bosses understand other men's emotions, as they have been through these themselves. They don't understand how a woman feels, as they have never been a woman. So life gets tough early on. Women do not always appreciate that, in joining a male-dominated company or profession, they have entered a foreign country where they may not know the language, or have any maps.

It is only by living in that country, and being eternally vigilant, that you gradually come to learn the rules. You will only ever obtain promotion by playing the same game as men, rather than by being so good at your work that your excellence is noted. A book that has become a classic of its kind is *The Managerial Woman*, by Margaret Hennig and Anne Jardim. This book underlines the need to be very aware of male strategies, if you are bent on securing promotion for yourself.

A woman is still, to a very large extent, an unknown quantity in office life. True, men see women at home and sitting at typewriters, but they don't, on the whole, see them in positions of responsibility. You have to *prove* your worth to them, and make them see that you are worthy of promotion. Hennig and Jardim say:

The first step [in securing promotion] lies in accepting that the residues of difference will remain with us for the rest of our lives. A woman may always be anxious over the potential conflict between being a higher achiever and a successful woman. She may always be vulnerable to criticism in a way that is more directly personal than it is for men. She may always see career risk as a little more dangerous. She may always find it difficult to be aggressive and to initiate her own cause. These residues will remain. They need to be identified and managed. Situations which bring them back in strength need to be anticipated and planned for and one needs to practice at the lower end of the scale so that gradations can be consciously established in what represents conflict, vulnerability, risk, aggressiveness.

The second step is the most critical of all. It is the decision whether one really wants to succeed in a management career, a career that requires competing primarily with men, and competing with them in a system they understand better and on terms with which they are far more comfortable and much more familiar.

A woman must be able to say with confidence that she wants a career and that she is willing to confront the problems she will inevitably encounter. She must be willing to be far more specific in her planning than the men around her, and even more alert at anticipating situations which might accentuate the pressure she will feel or expose the vulnerabilities she will continue to sense. She must in other words be clear on the need to manage her environment and herself concurrently.

(*The Managerial Woman*, pp.157-159.)

So how do you set about putting yourself in line for promotion? First, by being confident enough to apply for jobs when they come up. Too many women tend to sit back and wait to be promoted. But that will never happen. Next, you must make yourself noticed, learn who is leaving and who is staying, and also get to know the office structure intimately. In many big companies, as with the armed forces, there are definite time-scales on each ladder. For example, in the Army you are usually made a Major at around your thirtieth birthday, and it is unusual to get that position much earlier or much later. So it is in corporations. You should have reached a certain rank by a certain time and if you haven't, further promotion may be out of the question.

What usually happens with a large firm is that there is a very definite structure and you must, at an early stage, get to know this. You must also be aware of the qualities needed to become a manager. The most essential of these is the ability to delegate. Women can be notoriously bad at this, and you often find female office managers continuing to do the typing and shorthand because they came top in this at secretarial college, and don't trust anybody else to do the job as well.

You must be willing to let your previous job go once you have secured another higher up the tree, and this is something women can find hard.

You should, if at all possible, try to make friends with another woman higher up the management level, if there is one. Executive women have often been accused of pulling the ladder away from underneath them when they have reached the top, rather than lending a helping hand to other women who want to climb the same path. Some women are like this – a feeling of solidarity among women is not encouraged in many firms, and for centuries women have been used to competing with each other for male attention, rather than climbing together for their own good – but women have to learn that they have nothing to lose and everything to gain by banding together. This builds bridges for other women to cross and creates a network which can only be helpful to other women entering the field.

But as yet, the 'Queen Bee' syndrome is all too prevalent among women, and it is caused mainly by insecurity at being in a man's world. Some women really do enjoy being the only female on the board, or at the top of the pecking order. It is for the present generation to understand that life actually becomes easier and pleasanter for all when there are more women at the top. It helps to redress the imbalance that has pervaded business and professional life for so long.

Men have to realize that they have nothing to lose, and women have much to gain as well, when more women are promoted to influential positions. Of course, one token woman can't change the office structure, but lots of women all the way up the hierarchy can, very significantly. As the sexes become more equal in the world of work, suspicion and mistrust of each other will start to disappear.

Very often, when you are up for a higher job, you will find yourself before an all-male selection panel. It could be difficult to persuade them that you are the 'man' for the job, particularly if the men doing the choosing have homebound wives and mothers, apparently happy enough in the domestic role.

There is also a feeling that, whenever there is a shortage of jobs, it is quite all right for the women to be passed over. If you are inexplicably passed over for the job – it is rare for selection panels to tell you just why they did not consider you suitable – you have every right to request an explanation. Employers do not have to tell you why you were not picked, but if you ask embarrassing questions, it may make them review their tactics in future. Many men have the attitude that women don't *mind* so much as men if they are passed over, or are earning less, or are less highly regarded. They can still be well thought of *for a woman*, the assumption goes. Sometimes, when asking why you were not chosen, you get evasive answers such as: 'We're not sure how the sales force would react to a woman', or 'These boys aren't used to having a woman in charge.' If you hear answers like these, it could be that your promotion chances are effectively blocked, in that particular firm.

If this is the case, it would be wise to look for a job with another company without delay. You can always return to your present company at a later date, if they then offer you the job you seek. You can suddenly find you become very desirable when you leave your company to go to another, at a higher salary. One colleague went for a rise, and was told this was impossible at the present time, blah, blah, blah. She found herself another job, straight away at a considerably higher salary. Within a year, her previous firm were wooing her back with salary offers beyond the dreams of avarice.

You must always be prepared to take your fate into your own hands, and not just hope that you will be in line when the next promotions are made. Don't ever be defeated by early setbacks as these happen to us all. The more you are, the more likely you are in fact to encounter setbacks, particularly in the early stages of the career climb.

Dame Josephine Barnes, formerly consultant gynaecologist at the Charing Cross Hospital (now retired), decided soon after she qualified that she wanted to become a consultant at a London teaching hospital. In the event, it took her twenty-five years to attain that position, long after most men who had qualified at the same time. She found she was being turned down again and again, for no good reason. She had proved her commitment to the job by working right through having two children. But none of this deterred her. She kept applying for job after job until, eventually, she was offered the one she wanted. Because her vision was so clear, and undeflected by reversals of fortune, she eventually achieved her ambition, and so can you. Whatever you want you can have – so long as you really want it. You won't rise in a company as a protest against the ill-treatment of women – you have to absolutely want it for yourself, and make up your mind that nothing will stand in your way.

This doesn't mean you must be dishonest, or revert to shady business practices. Far from it. It simply means you must keep your eventual goal in sight, whatever might happen along the way.

Nearly all ambitious women working in hierarchical professions find that, somewhere along the line, their way will be blocked by men who are not keen to promote a female. They may give rational-sounding reasons for not wanting women, but it is actually fear that stops them. All the traditional professions, such as the Civil Service, law, medicine, local government, employ very many women indeed, but almost all of them are on the lowly rungs of the ladder. If you expect that, at some stage your promotion is likely to be blocked, at least you will be ready to meet this, rather than have it take you by surprise.

And when it happens, you can have your strategy all ready. Apply, and apply and apply, and reapply if necessary. Teach your employers that you are in deadly earnest.

Then, if you keep meeting the same brick wall, you should look for another post. This was amusingly illustrated in the comedy series *Yes Minister*, referred to in the last chapter. A senior civil servant, played by Eleanor Bron, was having difficulty securing promotion, 'because her children might get measles'. She retaliated by securing herself a job as director of a merchant bank, and the token woman was lost.

Men are frightened that, if women were suddenly let in in large numbers, they might twig as to what was really going on – about how, in so many jobs, work is extended infinitely by 'meetings', and how pieces of paper are shuffled to and fro, in an attempt to seem busy and important. That is, I'm sure, the real reason women aren't promoted. The men are afraid of being found out.

But not all top jobs are as portrayed in *Yes, Minister*, where constant time-wasting tactics are employed to stop anything at all from ever being done. There may be an element of truth in this, in local government and Civil Service jobs, but in competitive industries results must be seen, otherwise the firm will rapidly go out of business. There is little room for time wasting in big multinational companies. So, if you expect promotion in one of these, you must actually be prepared to work very hard. It's no use expecting to clock off on the dot of five, or have every weekend free for gardening or embroidery. If you want to get to the top, your job must really be your life – not necessarily the whole of it, but certainly a very important part.

Not everybody, men or women, have this level of commitment, and there is no reason why they should. But commitment is essential to rise, in any profession whatsoever, where large salaries are among the rewards.

There are two other ingrained and entrenched female attitudes that tend to stop women from being promoted. One is that many are simply not interested in the power games that are played by men – the big desks, the transatlantic phone calls, the hastily-convened meetings, the big lunches, the entourage of secretaries and assistants. Women who do not find this game fascinating will never be promoted very far. You have to be a political animal, and actually enjoy the cut and thrust of office politics, at the same time realizing that it is a game people play. Don't ever take it to heart. It's all like a big game of monopoly, or chess. And ruthlessness – or single-mindedness as I prefer to call it – is an absolute essential.

If you find that, after a few years struggling to come to terms with large companies, you still do not have the foggiest idea of the underlying philosophy that makes big business tick, you may simply not be suited to this life. You may be better off with a far smaller company or, indeed, in setting up your own concern. Women are spectacularly successful at setting up their own businesses. You can read more about how to do it in Chapter Six.

The other hampering attitude is that so many women feel so profoundly grateful to be employed at all. Women architects and doctors, working on low rungs of the ladder, often feel so glad that they have managed to get anywhere at all, and this feeling of gratitude stops them from clambering further up. Others, perhaps in less demanding jobs, are hampered by a feeling of loyalty to their boss, or to the firm. You meet so many middle-aged secretaries, who have been with their present boss for over 20 years and feel he would fall apart if they left. These women have effectively put their own blocks on their careers. The important person in all this is you, not some boss.

The only loyalty you should have is to yourself, as nobody else is worth it. This doesn't mean you have to betray people and keep letting them down, simply that you should not put anybody else's career or wishes before your own.

Do not over-identify with your firm to such an extent that you feel you can never leave. On the whole, you do tend to find that those who have been longest with the same company are the lowest paid. The high fliers and the high earners are prepared to move often. Being prepared to uproot and change jobs when the challenge is over, is a sign of seriousness about your career. Not that you should move simply for the sake of moving, as this can make you feel unsettled and unsure of your place in the world. A job must always be more than simply promotion prospects, otherwise you are forever living in the future.

There are times in everybody's career pattern when an apparent ceiling has been reached, and it can be wise to stay put for a bit and consolidate, sometimes. And the higher you go, the less likely you are to be on the move. Constant motion in jobs is for the young execs, the under-35s.

A word here again about being a secretary: if you are in your mid to late twenties, it really is time to start thinking about doing something else. After the age of 35, when executives start to find their professional feet, a secretary can discover her days are numbered. A quick look at ads for secretaries reveals that few are wanted after age 35. That is also when salary levels are at their highest: after this age, they tend to go down again, and your employability diminishes. Few people – men at least – like a middle-aged secretary. A young man of 28 may find it rather hard to issue orders to a woman of 48, old enough to be his mother. So the solution tends to be for him to get rid of the mother-figure and employ more of a young thing instead.

Many courses and opportunities now exist to up your skills, and become a manager instead of a secretary. Eleanor Macdonald, now in her seventies, and a former executive with a large department store, has pioneered such seminars in her now famous EM Courses.

Here, would-be female managers are taught to come to terms with the male dominance at work, to understand it, and to learn much needed self-confidence. Many hundreds of women have taken these courses, which are often paid for by the firms themselves.

NOWME – the National Organization for Women's Management Education – also runs courses and weekends for those women who want to know the secrets of getting into managerial positions. Here is one woman's experience of attending a NOWME course at Cranfield College, Bedford: 'I looked forward to the Personal and Career Development Weekend at Cranfield with some trepidation – I felt the prospect of spending a whole weekend with a group of women might be a bit of a trial. Firmly fixed in my mind was a picture of a stereotypical intense female executive twice as competitive as any man, with a cutting edge which would make a guillotine look blunt.' (As you see, even women have a negative picture of women at the top.) She concluded: 'I gained some very useful insights into myself, such as how to market my experience positively, in letters of application and CVs, how to be positive about my achievements, especially in an interview. Another "plus" was being able to work out how to deal assertively with an awkward senior male colleague.'

NOWME also operates as a resource centre, and pools details of courses for would-be women managers, which are aimed at making women more effective and less nervous in the business world. Things are improving, but you may still have to make that extra effort to push yourself into a proper career structure.

One very welcome development that has helped many aspiring women in recent years has been the rise of women-only professional associations. Here, those who are serious about their jobs can meet and discuss issues that affect their work. Women have not been, on the whole, greatly attracted to trade unions, but women's networks are now becoming very popular in Britain, America and Australia.

There now exists (not a complete list) the Women's Engineering Society, Women in Manual Trades, Women in Banking, Women in the Civil Service, Medical Women's Federation, Women in Entertainment, Women in Publishing, Women in Media. These associations all look at possible promotion bias, and to try to work out ways of combating it.

There is also Network, as association of executive and managerial women started in 1981 by Irene Harris. The qualification for membership is that you have to have been in an executive position for the past two years. Talks, seminars and weekends are held, all with the purpose of improving women's lot in the professional world. *Network* is expanding fast, and now has a formidable list of high-earning and successful members.

If you feel you would like to get on in your career, but can't see how to do it, it would be worth booking yourself onto one of these courses, and getting some specific gen. NOWME have details of most of the women's management and career courses taking place in various parts of the country.

Further Reading and Information

The Managerial Woman, by Margaret Hennig and Anne Jardim (Marion Boyars, 1978).

The Cinderella Complex: Women's Hidden Fear of Independence, Colette Dowling (Fontana, 1982).

Subject Women, Ann Oakley (Fontana, 1981).

EM Courses, 4 Mapledale Avenue, Croydon, Surrey. Send sae for information.

National Organization for Women's Management Education (NOWME), Lene Orchard, 29 Burkes Road, Beaconsfield, Bucks.

Network, Irene Harris, 8 Thornton Place, London W1H 1FC.

300 Group (For more women in parliament), Lesley Abdela, 2 The Old Kiln, Nettlebed, Henley-on-Thames, Oxfordshire.

Federation of Business and Professional Women, 54 Bloomsbury Street, London WC1 3QU.

3

The Working Mother

It used to be the case that you had to leave work when you got married. Now the great divide between a working and non-working life, at least in the economic sense, seems to threaten when children come along. Though there is no law saying you have to leave work when pregnant, many women automatically think they must hand in their notice at this stage, and not even consider returning to work until the children are at school.

This is a dangerous assumption for any career-minded woman to make as, the longer you leave it, the more difficult it becomes to get back to work at all, let alone in the position you left. Machinery may have taken over your original job, the office junior may have been promoted to a position above you, or all your former colleagues may have moved on. The firm itself might have gone out of existence. After spending several years at home, you are unlikely to be considered a very good employment prospect anyway.

So, any woman who thinks of her work as more than just a fill-in between leaving school and having children, should very carefully consider her career position before ever becoming pregnant. All the pro and cons should be weighed up, and wherever possible, pregnancy embarked on at just the right time for you, your career, and your future prospects.

No woman *has* to have a baby, of course, but most, whether working or not, feel the urge at some time in their lives. The American feminist Betty Friedan has, in her book *The Second Stage* (Michael Joseph, 1982), spoken of the 'baby urge' that won't go away. According to Betty, the great majority of women still want to have families of their own, regardless of whether or not they have careers.

It is not always so simple to see how to fit these children into a career pattern, or to envisage what kind of disruption a family might cause. For my part, I believe that the difficulties of combining a job with bringing up a family have been greatly over-exaggerated, and nowadays any woman who wants to can perfectly well do both. In the days when babies came uninvited and a woman could expect to conceive at least 10 times in her life, things were very different. But now, babies can often be planned with meticulous precision, and timed to fit in with a working life.

In most jobs, you do not have to make a choice about whether to have children or continue as a career girl. The two are by no means mutually exclusive and in the immortal words of American *Cosmopolitan* editor Helen Gurley Brown, herself childless it must be admitted, you can 'have it all'. And nobody need suffer in the process, neither you, your husband, your children or your job. In fact, most homes are enhanced, rather than the opposite, by a working mother.

But in order to do it all properly, rather than muddling through and lurching from one crisis to the next, precision planning is needed. Before you start to make practical plans, you should also realize that the only things really standing in the way of a woman having it all are the negative emotions of guilt, worry and fear. As soon as you decide to banish these monsters from your life, the dark clouds will lift, and you will immediately have shaken off a heavy burden of useless mental and emotional lumber.

When I had young children and went off to work I tended, as did most working mums in those days, to feel guilty. This was mainly because I enjoyed my work so much more than looking after little children. But I stopped feeling guilty the minute I read a book by American psychologist Wayne Dyer, called *Your Erroneous Zones* (Sphere, 1977), which underlines exactly how pointless guilt is. What does it ever achieve, Dr Dyer asks, and where does guilt get you?

It is caused by anxiety about past actions which can never, whatever the consequences, be altered. Guilt is debilitating and ageing, and is liable to affect the working mother with young children more than any other section of society. Once you make up your mind to banish guilt from your life, as I did, the rest becomes comparatively easy.

The right time
Granted that most women do, at some stage, want to have children, when is it best to take the plunge? Unfortunately, the way work is geared these days, the promotional ladder is usually being climbed between the ages of 25 and 35, which is exactly when most women want to have their babies. The ages outside this ten-year span are less ideal, for many reasons. Younger than 25, you probably haven't got yourself or your life together, and older, you may wonder whether it is too late. It is really a matter of choosing the optimum time within this age range, and this very much depends on the type of job you hold, what the prospects are, and how much a pregnancy is likely to alter your chances of promotion and seniority. Before ever embarking on a pregnancy, take a long, hard look

at your career, ask yourself what you want out of it, how you are likely
to achieve this, and how children would fit in.

If your job entails a great deal of travel, it could be difficult to
combine this with a family, but you may be able to change direction
towards a more office-based job in the same area. I'm thinking here of
couriers, air hostesses, or those working on shipping lines. Instead of just
giving up and giving in your notice on becoming pregnant, first find out
which more stationary jobs would be available.

It may, of course, be the right time for you to pack in your present
career and embark on another, which will need a further period of
training. In which case, this is an ideal time to have a baby, as young
children fit in very well with obtaining further qualifications. Many
colleges now have creches and playgroups, and you may be able to
obtain a grant while studying.

But whatever you do, it is important to think ahead, rather than hope
some happy solution will just present itself – it won't. If you wait to see
what happens, nothing will.

But if you do decide to take a course of further study, it should ideally
lead to something concrete, rather than being a method of filling in
otherwise 'dead' time. A course taken simply for the hell of it may lead
to a good job later, but this is unlikely. On the other hand, something
you fancy the idea of, such as pottery, for example, could lead you into
starting up your own crafts business. There should always be some end in
view, even if things don't work out exactly as planned. A course or
degree taken with a definite purpose always has the edge, and in fact, is
far more enjoyable than one taken because you can't think of anything
else to do.

What, you may ask, if you get pregnant accidentally? Well, I don't
believe that a responsible career woman ever does become pregnant as
the result of an accident. At some level, even the deeply unconscious
one, she wants it to happen. And if she does conceive, it's for some
reason, however irrational it may seem. It is true that some people,
however intelligent, like to have conscious responsibility taken away
from them. I don't recommend an 'accidental' pregnancy as a wise
course of action for the committed career girl. It will throw everything
into confusion, and may upset your life for many years to come.
Remember that children are an 18-year responsibility, and a long, long
commitment. After you have them, your life will never be the same
again, whether you are a full-time working mother or not.

I meet so many women, of all ages, who hate their lives because they
feel so useless and purposeless and rudderless. They are the ones who
discover that having children has not brought them the fulfilment they
expected.

Expectations of motherhood

It is true that some women are natural mothers, who love children and ask for nothing more out of life than to have dozens of them. Such women are, though, a comparative rarity and, I suspect, always have been. Also, there are women who do not want to work and earn a living and are far happier being at home all day. But if this is not you, you should not try to pretend that it is, or attempt to live up to some impossible ideal of motherhood. You feel how you feel, regardless of whether or not these are the 'right' emotions somebody says you should be having.

You do not have to have a baby to find out if you are likely to find full-time homemaking and childcare fulfilling as a permanent way of life. You simply have to ask yourself, well before C-day, whether you actually enjoy domestic pursuits, and think back to whether, as a child yourself, you enjoyed playing with dolls, looking after teddies, or pushing prams. If so, you probably have strong maternal instincts. Perhaps you like looking after people, or doing things for them when they are ill. In which case, you will very likely enjoy motherhood as well.

But if not, you shouldn't be surprised to find that you can't enjoy it very much at all. Just because you possess the biological equipment that allows you to reproduce, it doesn't automatically follow that you are one of nature's childbearers and looker-afterers, with everything else in your life taking second place.

Children do not and cannot bring 'fulfilment', because they are not part of you. They are external, separate human beings with their own personalities, interests and behavioural patterns. Any woman who tries to view her children as an extension of herself is doomed to eventual disappointment, because the day will come when they will let her down, or want to escape permanently.

Western life is geared so that non-working mothers with small children tend to lead very isolated lives. Small children are not very welcome in restaurants, hotels, on buses or department stores. Germaine Greer has called our society 'profoundly anti-child', and she has a point. This isolation will be your lot too, unless you take very definite steps to prevent it. You will be isolated unless you consciously plan not to be.

But maternity and parenthood need not upset your career, not even cause it the merest hiccup, so long as the right amount of forward planning is brought to bear on the whole issue. As pregnancy usually takes two (though in these days, it isn't always the case), do discuss the whole thing in depth with your partner, and gauge his attitude. Does he want a baby equally as much as you? If so, how much effort is he prepared to put in on the caring side? Any partner who doesn't seem keen will not magically change when the tiny infant is put into his arms, so don't expect a non-helper to turn suddenly into a helper.

Finances

What about the financial side? If you reckon you would like a couple of years off – and many careers can stand a break of this length – it's not a bad idea to save for this eventuality well in advance, so that you continue to have an income of your own in the meantime. I'm an advocate of saving up for all the worthwhile things in life, rather than merely living from hand to mouth. It is a fact that today's women can take the loss of personal income that not working entails very hard indeed, even when it is temporary.

Some money of your own in the bank can make a very real difference both to your self-esteem and your freedom. Women who hate the very idea of being dependent on another should not even entertain the idea of not working. It doesn't come any easier when it is an actuality.

That trapped feeling many mothers experience and speak of at length, comes mainly from not having an individual income. Nothing makes a woman feel more second-class and second-rate, or is calculated to engender childish, dependent, wheedling behaviour, than a nil income. When no women worked for money, and were not expected to, it was entirely a different matter. Now, though, the woman at home tends to see her wage-earning friends having a whole different attitude to money and relationships and is likely to feel distinctly envious.

When 'our' money is in reality his, and you both know it, your energy, self-confidence and self-esteem can take a terrible dive. The saddest thing of all I see these days, and it is something very much on the increase, is when a husband leaves his non-career, housewifely wife for a younger model who will usually be a career woman. I've seen it happen in all professions, and it's likely to become a bigger, not smaller, problem, as time goes on.

When this happens, the non-career wife can find herself in a very sorry state indeed. All that she has worked for and wanted goes in one fell swoop, as she no longer has a man to make her existence feasible. Only the other day, a friend contacted me to say that her husband had just left her, and she had now to try and earn her own living. A vicar's wife, used to a large house and prestige – if only vicarious – she was now reduced to living on social security. Ten years had passed since she last earned money: how on earth, she wondered, was she ever to get started again?

Clues to solving this dilemma will be given in Chapter Four, but in the meantime, don't, if possible, let this happen to you. Though one should not plan for a husband to walk off, you never know when it might happen. Such a prospect need not unduly worry you if you maintain your independence and this, as with everything else in life, comes from having the right attitude at the start.

In these days of at least theoretical equal opportunity and education, why should a man expect to keep a woman? And why should a woman not pull her weight financially? Come to that, why shouldn't a man put in an equal share domestically?

There is no God-given reason why not, and it is all possible. Few women want to walk through life alone and most, at some stage, either get married·or enter into a long-term relationship. This is not a marriage guidance book but any woman who wants to remain a person in her own right, and keep her career going should, ideally, marry a man whose career can fit in with hers. I feel the happiest marriages are made when two people are equally educated, have equal earning powers and similar jobs. That way, you become true partners and have plenty in common to keep you interested in each other for many years.

Because these days one cannot, in all honesty, regard bringing up a couple of children, however conscientiously it is done, as a full-time career, other plans should be made. In the days when many women had to cook, sew, spin and grow vegetables to ensure survival, another career would have been out of the question. Nowadays an 'idle' life without a good job is not a satisfactory solution, unless you come from the landed aristocracy, where a support network and a full, busy life is actually built into the class structure. That, however, is not for most of us, and never will be.

A conflict of interests

However, even in the best planned lives, surprises can happen. You may have worked everything out so that you decide now is the right time to have a baby. You are on top of your job, and feel it can be all plain sailing for a couple of years. Then the unexpected happens, and you are offered a big promotion, or a rival firm makes you an offer you would be mad to refuse. What to do? Should you back off, telling them you are pregnant, or what?

A man will obviously never have to face this difficulty, so should it be any different for you? My own inclination would be to accept the promotion, or new job if you would sincerely like the step up. But don't, whatever you do, try to keep the pregnancy a secret. When you are offered the job, say that you are three months pregnant (or whatever) but you still think you can do it. It may be that the job you are offered is impossible to combine with pregnancy, as it involves extensive travel. In this case, say you cannot take this particular job, but are keen to rise within the company. You may be able to discuss alternatives with your boss.

Most promotional jobs can, however, be combined quite easily with pregnancy. This very thing happened to two friends of mine, both of whom were two months pregnant at the time. One was offered a better job with another firm, where there had never before been a pregnant woman in the job, and the other friend was offered a big promotion. Both took a deep breath, and accepted the jobs, revealing at the same time that they were pregnant.

Neither were very young to be first-time mothers, as both were in their mid-thirties, and one was having to be carefully monitored for medical reasons. However, both found themselves perfectly well able to cope with the new jobs, and continue their pregnancies. Four years later, jobs and children are flourishing in both cases. Pregnancy does not adversely affect your brain, though it will inevitably slow you down physically as time goes on.

Some career women worry that it will not look very professional to be pregnant, particularly in a male-oriented profession. But the men there will soon get used to it – it won't stop them taking orders from you if you are in an executive position. Unless you feel embarrassed, they won't be – and they may even regard you as more human and approachable than before.

Maternity rights

The very real question of maternity leave, maternity pay and time off to attend antenatal clinics has to be faced, as has the possibility that you may not be feeling 100 per cent well throughout. You will, as soon as possible, have to work out with your boss exactly what time off you will need, and when you expect to be able to return. It is only courtesy to do this as soon as your pregnancy is confirmed, in case your company has to cover for you in your absence.

Also, find out as soon as you can what your firm's maternity rights are, as these may be more generous than the statutory government regulations. The Maternity Alliance provide a checklist for all employees, personnel officers and trade union representatives to consult, so there is no excuse for anybody not knowing what the position is. If you are an employee, you should ask your personnel officer, if there is one, for information about any negotiated maternity rights, and whether there are special provisions made. It is not a bad idea to find this out *before* you become pregnant, as this may affect your decision to leave, to stay, or to look for another job.

You must let your employer know when you are likely to be attending antenatal clinics. You have a statutory right to attend these. After the first appointment, you should be able to produce an appointment card, and certificate from your doctor or midwife or health visitor, stating that you are pregnant. To qualify for maternity pay and leave, you must normally have worked in the same firm full-time for at least two years, or part-time – that is, eight hours or more a week – for five years. You must also have paid full National Insurance Contributions. The 'married woman's option' to pay lower NI Contributions has now been stopped, so most younger working women will be paying the full amount.

The legal position is that you are entitled to six weeks' maternity leave at nine-tenths your normal wage, minus national insurance and the maternity allowance of £29 (1985 figure). You will get this anyway – every mother does. You should have completed the required years of service by the beginning of the 11th week before the expected week of confinement. You must also, by law, write to your employer at least 21 days before stopping work, to say you are leaving to have a baby, also giving the expected week of confinement, and the date you expect to return. Don't ever say you expect to return if in fact you have no intention of so doing. Such deception gets women a bad name in the workplace.

Other statutory rights are: if your firm has more than five employees you will be entitled to return up to 29 weeks after the birth. That is, unless, for some very good reason, it is impractical for your job to be held open for you. It is the employer's job, not yours, to arrange for temporary cover, if necessary. After the baby is born, you should write to your employer, confirming your intention to return to work. This must be done at least three weeks beforehand, and if you don't do this, you may find your job has been taken. You will have no right of redress.

These are the minimum rights laid down by law, but your firm may well have better ones. If it is a large company, it very probably will have agreed its own maternity deal, which would be an improvement on the minimum rights. Any firm that is keen to encourage women will very likely have a good maternity scheme, but one which wants to turn them away may abide by the minimum.

Pregnancy is not an illness, and should not be treated as such. Current medical thinking believes it is actually far better to keep working than to put your feet up for the whole nine months. The growing baby will not suffer, so long as you are in good health, and don't overdo it.

But any sign of continuing high blood-pressure, swelling of legs or ankles, may indicate that you should stop working earlier than originally intended. In this case, you may qualify for sick, rather than maternity leave. There is no evidence at all that working at a paid job heightens your chances of having a miscarriage, though a longer than average working week, working on an industrial conveyor belt, and jobs which require physical rather than mental effort, are all likely to increase chances, according to Ann Oakley in her book *Miscarriage*. If you have a family history of miscarriage it might be a wise decision to take some time off in the early months, when miscarriages are more likely to occur.

If you feel perfectly well, there is nothing wrong with working right up until the very week of the birth. The time you will really appreciate off is after the baby is born, as then you will have some very major adjustments to make that could cause strain and stress, as well as tiredness. It all depends on how you, as an individual, feel. Some women manage to keep working up to the very day of birth without ill effects, either to themselves or to the baby. Margaret Ghilchik, one of the very few women general surgeons in Britain, said that she worked right up to the birth of each of her four children, and was back in each case six weeks later. *And* she had two of her children when in her forties.

If you don't expect to be ill or feel uncomfortable, then you will very probably sail through the whole nine months. This can't be absolutely guaranteed, though! The best thing is to listen carefully to what your body is trying to tell you, as every woman has a different degree of robustness and capacity to take strain. Mental strain at work should not hurt the baby, but if your job is very physical, you may like to consider packing it in earlier. Jobs that involve a lot of driving and travel, for example, may have to be stopped sooner than more sedentary occupations.

As a general rule, work as long as you can. Very, very single-minded mothers are apt to be found sitting up in their hospital bed writing articles or reading company reports less than 24 hours after delivery – I was one of these – but don't feel you *have* to. There is no need to be Superwoman about it, and most jobs can wait for a few weeks before you give them your attention again.

The feminist writer and psychologist Susie Orbach, author of *Fat is a Feminist Issue*, decided at the age of 37 that she wanted to have a baby. Determined to do the whole thing properly, she and her partner saved up enough money to enable each of them to take six months off work to concentrate full-time on the baby. Her partner actually took six months' unpaid paternity leave – something other men may like to consider.

If you feel you would like to take more than the statutory time off, and your firm has not negotiated any extra benefits for its female staff, you may be able to take some extra unpaid leave. All this would need detailed discussion beforehand, of course.

Paternity leave is slowly coming in, as more firms are giving some slight provision to fathers. Some countries now have statutory agreements for new fathers to have up to a week off following the birth, but there is no such arrangement in Britain yet. It must be said that Britain's men are not pressing especially hard for paternity leave. One male editor of a woman's magazine, whose firm have just introduced paternity provision, said: 'You wonder, do you have to take it?'

But fathers should have time off around the birth. The weeks following delivery, particularly when the midwife and health visitor stop coming, are the most valuable. Your partner should find out from his firm whether there are any paternity arrangements, and decide well ahead of time what leave he will take. It does help if, right from the start, you see bringing a new life into the world as a joint venture.

All too many men still consider bringing babies into the world and raising children as 'women's work'. Women themselves must teach the men that this isn't so, and if you are considering embarking on your first pregnancy, then now is a good time to start.

At the moment, about half of all pregnant women in Britain are in paid work, and between two-thirds and three-quarters are employed up to 28 weeks or more. So nobody will think you odd if you carry on with a big bulge in front.

The next six months
The time leading up to the birth is not usually a problem. About 80 per cent of all women sail through pregnancy, and you may well find you feel even better, happier and fitter than before. It is after the birth that you could, if you are not very careful, find that your career goes completely haywire. Most, but by no means all, new mothers discover that they are very taken indeed with the tiny creature they have just produced, and may feel they could not possibly go back to work in a hard-headed, business-like office, now that they have this little human to care for.

This feeling, though, rarely lasts beyond the first six months, so anybody who is astonished by the strength of their maternal feelings should wait for these to subside somewhat before making any irrevocable decisions. So many women who decide to give up work when their baby is a week old bitterly regret it later and find that, when they do eventually try to go back to work, doors have mysteriously closed, or they have missed out on important seniority, and would have to restart at a lower position.

If you are overcome with the joys of motherhood, and think that life at home isn't as bad as some have painted it, do wait until you are properly back on your feet before making a decision that could effectively kill your career. You may feel, after a few months have passed, that your desire to return to work has not been renewed. In this case, you should carefully assess the situation, and try to work out what you would like to do instead. Because, if you are reading this book, you will probably not be satisfied with staying at home for very long.

You may be quite determined that you want to go back to work, but are worried about two important aspects: breastfeeding and childcare. There is no doubt at all that breastfeeding is the very best gift you can ever give your baby. It is also best for you because it, as it were, completes the circuit of childbirth, and allows the proper hormones to circulate as they should. Breastfeeding also allows the uterus to contract and helps you regain your pre-baby figure quickly. I notice that nearly all model girls are breastfeeding now, and finding that it doesn't spoil their figures in the least. Breastfed babies look nicer, smell nicer and behave more reasonably than bottle-fed ones. They are very likely to be healthier and, I'm sure, have nicer personalities.

Some dedicated career women feel they must get their babies onto the bottle as quickly as possible, otherwise a speedy return to work will be difficult. But this is not the case. The first six weeks or so are the vital ones, and if you can feed your baby for that length of time, you needn't worry so much about doing it for longer. As time goes on, your milk will decrease enough to enable you to breastfeed your baby and cope with a full day's work. If you can, ease yourself back into work gently, first by doing one day, then two, and gradually working up to a full week. You can only request, not demand, this but employers are often amenable to a staggered return. Working will not, in itself, decrease the milk supply and you are actually likely to be less tired when breastfeeding than if you are having to make bottles up all the time. Also, the baby will be more contented, and sleep better if breastfed.

Maire Messenger, author of *The Breastfeeding Book*, gives the following advice for women wanting to return to work while still feeding:

> At about two months, you can establish a routine whereby you feed the baby as late as possible in the morning, and then again as late as possible at night, say 6-7 a.m., and 8.30 p.m. This should ensure the baby goes through the night. It is wise to get the baby used to sucking on the bottle before you go back, and this will not put him off the breast provided you make sure he has the bottle only twice or three times a week. Your body will soon settle down to making enough milk for the daily feeds, but it may be useful to carry a breastpump with you to work, to express off any excess during the lunch hour.

Many mothers, says Maire Messenger, carry on working and breast-feeding successfully for up to a year and, in fact, far more successfully than mothers who don't work. It is the case that more working than non-working mothers actually do breastfeed these days. The impetus of having a job to go back to seems to sharpen up everything, making you more alive, alert and responsibly-minded. Babies are very good at picking up signals from their mother, and if a mother is happy and content, the baby will be too. They are accurate little reflectors of an adult state of mind.

Postnatal depression, that very common condition that can set in a week or so after the baby's birth, is also much less likely to happen if the baby is seen as a positive addition to your life rather than the beginning of the end of independent existence. I have the distinct impression that career-minded women are far less liable than stay-at-home ones to suffer from baby blues. This may be because they know more where they are going, and tend to be more sensible about organizing their lives. The new mother who sees each day stretching out endlessly in front of her, punctuated by baby yells or dreary chores, is very likely to succumb to bad fits of depression.

Postnatal depression may be hormonal, but what causes the hormones to bring about misery? The complex interaction of mind and body is nowhere more marked than just after the birth of a baby.

New mothers, whether career-minded or not, often worry about being tired, and are frightened at the sheer mess and drudgery a baby entails. In our capacity, we protect and look after the pregnant woman endlessly, but as soon as the baby is two weeks old, the midwife and health visitor disappear, husband goes back to work, and she is left, perhaps for the first time in her life, entirely alone.

Very often, she doesn't even know her immediate neighbours. This eventually should be realized in advance, and planned for long before the birth takes place. The National Childbirth Trust have many support groups for new mothers, and you should, if at all possible, join such a group, or perhaps establish one, so that there are no long days of loneliness and frustration. Get to know all the women in your locality who attend the antenatal classes, and resolve to keep in touch, at least for a bit, after the birth. This is very necessary, as it provides a bridge between the baby's arrival and your return to the outside world.

Childcare arrangements

If you are fully intent on going back to work again, you will have to make sure your childcare arrangements are adequate. Here, there is a variety of possibilities, and each of these depends on your circumstances, finances, and personal choice. Women in high paying jobs, earning at least £15,000 a year, will almost certainly opt for a full-time, live-in nanny. At one time it was quite difficult to obtain good nannies, but times have changed, and it has again become a popular job for young girls to do. One friend says she has only to whisper that her present nanny is leaving, to be besieged by phone calls. She's not a fabulously rich lady who lives in splendour and surrounded by servants, but a hardworking business executive in a fifth-floor London flat.

It's just that nowadays nannying is seen as a pleasant job, and its earlier connotations of servanthood have disappeared. In most modern career homes – I'm not talking about the upper echelons of the aristocracy where the nanny has an under-nanny – employees and nannies usually call each other by first names, and have a very matey relationship indeed. A quick call to a nanny training college or agency will give an idea of how much you can expect to pay per week, and what kind of working conditions a trained nanny would want.

Usually, she would have her own room, and not do any housework or washing except that directly connected with the baby. Nannies will, on the whole, prefer to take over the sole charge of your child, because this is what they have been trained to do.

Writer Mel Lewis and his wife, a teacher, had recurring childcare problems. They weren't happy with the babyminder and a Knightsbridge, London, nanny agency was asking £92 a week. The Lewises found the perfect solution by advertising in *The Lady* thus:

> NANNY – some experience preferred. Live in, weekends are yours. Own room, decorated to suit you, colour TV. Two bathrooms, use car. Responsive boy, 2. Teacher mum, writer dad. Pretty house near Islington, north London. Phone any time.

This ad brought 150 replies, and the Lewises interviewed 30 girls. Of these, 5 were suitable. Their ad cost £23.50 to place. Mel Lewis feels it's best to place a meticulously-worded ad, saying exactly what you want. The current (1985) rate for a live-in nanny is between £30 and £60 a week. If you look at *The Lady*, you will get a good idea of what is being offered to nannies nationwide. If your nanny earns more than £34 a week, you will have to tell the taxman, who will put her on to PAYE.

Some new mothers may feel nervous that the nanny will know more about babies than they do, and will want to take over completely. Well, that is the nanny's job, and she will expect to have a certain amount of autonomy. Nannies usually hate mothers to be around during the daytime, and are far happier if their employers actually go out to work. To obtain the right nanny, you must think carefully beforehand about what type of girl is likely to fit in with your household, and have this firmly in mind when you go about recruiting your ideal help.

As with taking on any other kind of staff, if something at the back of your mind niggles 'no', however much your rational self feels she would be ideal, don't hire her. Obey your intuition, even if you can't easily explain your feelings.

A trained nanny is almost a must for the new-born baby of a working mother, but you may decide to hire a specialized maternity nurse for the first month, rather than have a new nanny at this stage. Then the nanny can start later, when you have got used to the baby. Several career women I know have felt that a good, experienced maternity nurse was worth her weight in gold, and certainly worth foregoing their annual holiday for. After all, these women argued, you are pregnant only once or twice in a lifetime, so why not treat yourself, spoil yourself, and make the whole experience as pleasant as possible? Whether you are thinking about returning to work or not, you will need some sort of help for the first few weeks.

Modern women often find the mess and extra housework that a new baby entails extremely irksome, and it may also be worth your while engaging some domestic help, if only for a short time. Some women may worry that having a baby means they are suddenly having to take on a whole retinue of domestic staff, to do the jobs they used to manage perfectly well themselves, and wonder whether returning to work is worth the effort.

My answer to this would be yes, yes and yes again, for the following reasons: the retinue of domestic staff will decrease as the baby gets older and, also, having a baby will inevitably disrupt your life and mean major changes and adjustments. It may seem at first the easy and obvious solution to give up work, rather than go to the bother of hiring other people to look after your child and do your housework, but in the long term it becomes the more difficult path to choose, as it can mean the end of independent life. I very often hear women saying while sighing: 'I used to be as brainy and well-qualified as my husband, until I had the children. Then he sped ahead.'

The underlying resentment behind such words as these is not good for family or marital relationships. Such resentment is, however, very common with women who have allowed themselves to slip into a domestic kind of life without really thinking about what they are doing.

When you have been a long time out of work, your confidence evaporates, and this in itself, could hamper your getting back to your profession.

What if you want to return to work, but cannot possibly consider paying a full-time, trained nanny? There are other solutions. When I had my children, I couldn't afford either a maternity nurse or a nanny, and domestic help was out of the question, too. I had a complicated and reciprocal arrangement with friends, eked out by a babyminder. It was more difficult to arrange, but by no means impossible. So don't let the fact that you are not earning a fortune (a) put you off having a baby, or (b) lead you to imagine that it will not be possible to go back to work afterwards.

One acquaintance rang up the social services department where she lived and they gave her the name of a babyminder who looked after her child from the time it was three weeks old, and very effectively, too.

It may be that your workplace has a crèche, or there may be a nursery near you that takes newish babies. The local Citizens' Advice Bureau would have details, as would the antenatal and postnatal clinics.

These solutions would work out a lot cheaper than a live-in nanny, and the advantages are that your child would have other playmates. Also, a very real plus for some is that you wouldn't have to worry about what to do with the nanny at weekends. Most nannies like to take complete charge of the baby, and there can be clashes when you are at home together.

Or, you could share nanny with a working colleague, and halve the cost at the same time as providing an instant playmate for your child. To make this work, you would have to be in very regular working hours, and you and your friend would have to need the nanny absolutely equally. Share-a-Nanny schemes operate in many parts of the country, and if you don't actually know of a working mother in a similar situation to your own, the agency could put you in touch, and arrange matters to suit you both.

Another, even cheaper, solution is to find a reliable babyminder. This job used to be regarded in much the same way as a back-street abortionist, as a cheap and not very nice answer to the somewhat unwanted baby problem. Times have changed, though, and most professional babyminders these days are very nice women indeed, with children of their own. They have become very organized, and now have a national association, scale of fees and set working conditions. So long as you make sure you go to a proper registered babyminder, you should have no fears. Usually, you would take the baby to her, but she may prefer to come to your house instead.

You can expect that, whatever solution you finally arrive at, you will be less well off, financially, than before. A child always is a financial loss, and continues to be so for the next 18 years. Some mothers find that hiring help takes up practically all of their salary. I believe it is still worth working, even if *all* the salary does go, as the intense caring days are soon

over, and your salary will rise. In the meantime, you have remained a
working woman.

If you have a partner, do involve him in the childminding decisions. If
you are both equally working, you should be pulling equal weight on the
baby front as well, though this is by no means always the case. I think
here that many women have themselves to blame, as they can be very
possessive about the baby they have just produced, and exclude the
husband or partner. But don't take on all the responsibility and then start
complaining when he doesn't help out. If a man has grown up seeing
only women handle babies, and many have, it may simply not occur to
him to lend a hand. So, he must be gently taught and asked to change
nappies, take the initiative and help out of his own accord, at times.

This will not happen, of course, if you are a single parent. The
decision to go ahead and have a baby when you have no permanent
partner is one that more career women are now making. It is bold to
determine to do everything on your own, as the right partner does
undoubtedly ease the strain, but it is by no means impossible to do it by
yourself.

Indeed, very many married women with husbands who come home
every night in reality do bring the children up on their own. But if you do
not have the help of a committed partner you can expect to be even
worse off, financially, and be even more tired than if you could share the
strain with someone.

For single parents, the support network of friends is even more vital,
and should be sorted out as long as possible before the baby comes. You
may consider sharing a home with another single mother, pooling
resources, which always makes life easier. The main drawback of not
having a partner is having nobody to talk to, who has an equal interest in
the child. But single parenthood, any more than double parenthood,
does not have to mean the end of your career.

As the baby grows up, life becomes easier, and the support network
less essential. After a year, you would probably not need a fully trained
nanny, and can make do with a cheaper mother's help or au pair girl.
Many thousands of words have been written, and much anguish
expended, on the subject of au pairs. On the one hand, the girls
themselves often complain of being exploited, and on the other, the
employers complain that the girls are lazy, and forever making long-
distance calls to Dusseldorf or Madrid, or going out with unsuitable
boyfriends. Some women also worry in case their husbands take a fancy
to Ingrid or Maria, and end up in bed with her.

While examples can be found of horror stories – the latest and
nastiest one I heard was of an au pair's boyfriend stealing thousands of

pounds by forging the employee's signature on cheques – happy au pair arrangements are by no means uncommon. Some people prefer native mother's helps as they speak the same language, and will do at least some housework, while au pairs like to regard themselves as guests.

We tend to think it is difficult to obtain good childcare in this country, but in America, according to Susie Orbach, it is even worse. Hardly anybody wants to be a mother's help anyway, and you can't get foreign help because America is too far away from anywhere else.

Au pair girls are usually obtained via an agency, and there are firm regulations laid down as to the hours of work per week they should do, and what rates of pay they can expect. If you are not sure of the rates, look again in the working mother's Bible, *The Lady*, where you will see literally dozens of ads for domestic and childcare help. That will give you a clear idea of the kind of salary, or pocket money, you would have to provide.

I had foreign au pairs for years, and it worked out very well indeed. We found they added to, rather than detracted from, the atmosphere of the home, and my children benefitted from the extra input of interest. You sometimes hear that middle class children grow up unable to speak English properly because the only adult they communicate with all day is the foreign au pair, but this is just a 'new wives' tale', having no foundation in fact.

Before employing an au pair, you need to get straight, as with any other live-in help, exactly what will be your relationship with this, usually young, girl. Do you want her to eat with you, or not? Should she get up to prepare the children's breakfast? What about weekends? Do you mind her boyfriend coming in? Will she do shopping, cooking, ironing or housework, or not?

We had an au pair once who loved decorating and was often to be found up a ladder painting ceilings, when we came home from work. She also loved waxing parquet floors, but I must say, she was an extreme rarity, in this respect. Lazy girls are more the norm – think back to what you were like at the age of seventeen and remember your own attitude to domestic chores. Au pairs tend to have exactly the same attitudes.

In the early days of the women's liberation movement, radical feminists used to demand 24-hour nurseries. These haven't happened at all, partly owing to the sheer difficulty of arranging them, and partly because nobody ever took responsibility for setting these up. As your child gets older, a work crèche or babyminder may not continue to be the ideal answer and you may need to consider other forms of care if you are not keen, or are unable, to have somebody living in.

Day nurseries, which are intended for working mothers, usually run from about 8 a.m. to 5.30 or 6 p.m. including school holidays, and the good ones are a marvellous answer for mothers who don't want, or can't afford, live in care. The drawback is that they are few and far between. Ideally, you should find out the day nursery provisions in your area as soon as you know you are pregnant, and put your child's name down immediately. Good nurseries tend to be very booked up indeed, often for years ahead.

They are, or should be, run by qualified staff, who have gained the NNEB (National Nursery Examining Board) Certificate, and enjoy their work. Before actually putting your child's name down for a nursery, note the atmosphere, and whether the children all seem to be happy, lively and well catered for.

Playgroups are a different matter altogether. They are not intended for working mothers, as their hours are very short, with half terms and school-type holidays coming in as well. It's no good saying to yourself: 'I'll go back to work when my child is at playgroup', imagining that this will release you enough to return to a career. Usually, playgroups operate between 9.30 and 12.30, which hardly gives time to do any job at all, though they can be a godsend if you are doing part-time work at home. Playgroups exist mainly for the benefit of the children rather than the mother, and most working mums use them in addition to other types of care.

By the time your child is old enough to go to playgroup, though, the worst of your childcare worries will be over. Most groups take children when they are out of nappies at, say, two-and-a-half, and like to take them for two or three days a week before they go full time. It is not a good idea to try and combine a nursery with a playgroup, as this means too many different institutions and sets of people for a young child to get used to. A toddler attending playgroup would need either somebody at home all day, or to be sent to a childminder until you get home yourself.

The problems don't end with starting 'big' school, either. Many mothers who give up their careers when pregnant, say to themselves that they will go back to work when the youngest child is at school, then realize dismally that the children are at home for at least a third of the year. Infant school finishes at about quarter past three, then half terms, days off and holidays are for ever looming up.

Actually, you need to think in terms of substitute childcare until your child is about 11 or 12 years old, which is a very long time indeed. The amount of care and coverage needed does, though, get less as the years go by. It's worth thinking carefully about all this beforehand, as some women who at one time fully intended to return to work, find that this time is infinitely delayed, as the children always seem to need somebody to be around.

You would also need to do some pretty accurate financial considerations, to make sure childcare of one kind and another does not leave
you out of pocket. Playgroups run by mothers in their homes are fairly
cheap, but more professional ones, such as Montessori schools, can be
expensive. If you add this to your child-minding fees, plus evening
babyminding on occasion, you may actually find you are paying out
more than you bring home. As the very high-cost childcare is short
lasting, I would still feel it is worth making the financial sacrifice to hold
onto your job, especially as salary increases and promotions will more
likely come your way.

Working from home

Quite a few mothers feel that pregnancy is the time to make a break with
the past, and embark on a quite different kind of career, possibly
working from home. This, and setting up your own business, will be
examined more fully later, but a few words here may help to get the
matter into perspective. If your job is one that allows you to undertake
freelance commitments, the time to fix all this up is during the early days
of pregnancy, not when your child is several months old. Freelance
work, by its very nature, comes in fits and starts, and is often required at
short notice. Arranging child care on the spur of the moment may not be
so easy.

You would also have to find out whether there are genuine outlets for
your type of work, as this is not the case in every locality or every case.
If, for example, you have been a music teacher, and would like to
relinquish teaching in a school to give lessons at home, there are likely to
be plenty of pupils around.

But it wouldn't be so easy for a physics teacher to work from home.

Jobs that can successfully be carried on at home include: typing,
secretarial and translation work, indexing, proof-reading, pottery, and
all kinds of art. Working from home successfully does need both
business acumen and self-discipline. However talented you are, orders
will never just flood in as you sit by the phone. You have to sell yourself,
and be very professional about it, also charge the market rate for your
work. It is not fair, or good business sense, to undercut the market.

Women at home with small children can be prime targets for the
more exploitative types of homeworking, such as assembling Christmas
crackers, telephone selling, lingerie and other 'parties', or making toys.
You often see beguiling-looking ads in newspapers and magazines
asking whether you want to earn lots of money at home, and the
impression given is that you can become a millionaire, almost, by sitting
at home and working only a few hours a day. But anybody who

advertises 'work' is out to get your money, rather than give you any. These firms are not philanthropic organizations who would like you to get rich; they only want to get rich themselves.

I would very firmly beware of them. One of the very worst types of 'job', in my opinion, is telephone selling. Here, you have to phone up complete strangers in the evening, asking if they want double glazing, endowment mortgages or insurance policies. You will be taught a sales pitch, but it is very transparent. In most cases, you pay for all the telephone calls yourself, only earning when you actually make a sale. All that usually happens is that you find yourself with a mammoth telephone bill. Avoid these, and instead, look after other people's children, or go out cleaning – anything that avoids this awful exploitation, and putting money into other people's pockets.

As a general rule, take no notice at all of the so-called money-earning ads, as they end only in disappointment and bitterness. Nor am I at all in favour of clothes and goods 'parties' which also exploit the stay-at-home mother's wish to earn money at the same time as being with her children. I think these get-togethers are awful and embarrassing for everyone concerned – the woman who holds the party, and the friends who feel constrained to buy. If you do want to work, continue with a proper career or job structure, instead of getting mixed up with these dubious concerns.

Part-time work

You may feel that, while your children are very small, you would like to continue working for the same firm, but on a part-time basis. You have no automatic right to part-time work, and you could find you lose all your statutory rights, as well as bringing home so much less money. It may happen, though, that your firm are glad to employ you on a part-time basis, so do make enquiries if you don't imagine you can continue full-time work. Many more firms are now waking up to part-time possibilities, and you may be able to combine the hours with another part-time worker in a similar situation. Or you could try the comparatively new idea of job sharing. Again, the time to fix all this up is long before you actually have the baby, as it may be too late afterwards.

The concepts 'part-time' and 'full time' are very loaded, and may have little to do with actual hours worked. College lecturing is considered a full time job, yet some lecturers only 'work' 12 hours a week. Many part-time jobs would take up far more hours than this. Something to bear in mind is that women are very much associated with part-time work, and it can easily be another way of paying the female work force low wages. Hourly rates for part-time work are usually paid at the absolute minimum, and part-time work is often equated with a lack of commitment.

When considering part-time work, ask yourself whether you want to carry on with your career, or whether you just want a little bit of extra money and a little extra interest. These two very different attitudes to work will determine your approach. Do you see yourself primarily as a mother, or as a career woman first? A recent report commissioned by the Department of Health and Social Security discovered that most women would rather stay at home than be high-flying career girls.

They went out to work, the report suggested, mainly because they felt they needed the money. I'm sure the main reason why a large percentage of women felt that working was less preferable to being a wife and mother, was because most of them saw the jobs they did as boring, tedious and badly paid. This situation will never alter until women (a) decide to become better trained; (b) have a more positive attitude to work generally, and (c) think of themselves as independently-operating human beings, rather than adjuncts to a man.

If you are basically not a domestic person, and love the hustle and bustle of office life, being in charge, coping with challenges, looking smart and being efficient, it is unlikely that you will take very well to the essentially chaotic and muddly life of being a homebound mother. You will never be satisfied with trying to run your home on a time-and-motion basis, as homes and families simply don't admit to this kind of efficiency.

If you discover that you absolutely love making jam, daydreaming and sunbathing in the garden, having cosy chats with the neighbours and mooching round the shops, then you probably are more of a homebody. But there is no reason at all why a committed career woman shouldn't be a very successful mother as well, and the two are NOT mutually exclusive.

Too many women are still too timid about being in charge of their own lives, and imagine there is something sweet and feminine about being dependent. But you will not be doing either yourself or your relationship any good if you hide your light under a bushel, or suppress your career aims. There is never any need to be aggressive or arrogant – these qualities are unattractive in either sex – but don't think that it's wrong to earn more than your partner or husband, if yours is the greater talent, or better-paying job.

The greatest unhappiness lies in trying to be something you are not. By no means are all women domestically-minded mothers, and you will not be doing your children a favour by gritting your teeth, giving up your career and staying at home to look after them, if you are hating every minute of it. Unhappiness is quickly picked up by others, and it will affect the atmosphere of your home. Working mothers are always busy, but will not be more tired than stay-at-home ones, if they are content with their lives. Discontent is the greatest fatigue-maker.

Another aspect that bothers many women is worrying about what others might say. Some women have told me they wanted to go out to work with young children but that their mothers or mothers-in-law disapproved. But what has it got to do with them? Or your neighbours, or friends? Their disapproval doesn't make your decision wrong, and a lot of this apparent disapproval over working mothers is, in reality, envy. Your mother may tut-tut at you going out to work, because she remembers how she hated washing nappies at the kitchen sink. Your friends may gasp with envy when you go off to work, smartly dressed and made up every morning, while they are still slopping about in dressing gowns, and feel their day only begins when hubby arrives home from his office.

Nowadays, it is the working mother – so long as she is in an interesting job – who has a better life than the stay-at-home, non-working one.

Before ever handing in your notice because you are, or expect to be, pregnant, think very hard about all the options that are available to you, and what you can do with these options remembering that doors have a habit of clanging very firmly shut behind the stay-at-home mother with young children.

Good childcare *can* be arranged, so long as you take the trouble to work it all out beforehand. Your children will not suffer at all – in fact, they can often be better off for it. If mother is not around absolutely all the time, she becomes that little bit more special, and more appreciated. And more interesting as a mother.

Further Reading and Information

Miscarriage, Ann Oakley, Dr Ann McPherson and Helen Roberts (Fontana, 1984).
The Breastfeeding Book, Maire Messenger (Century, 1982).
What Do Women Want? Luise Eichenbaum and Susie Orbach (Fontana, 1984).

The National Childbirth Trust, 9 Queensborough Terrace, London W2.
Maternity Alliance, 309 Kentish Town Road, London NW5. (Information on maternity rights and services, plus leaflets on maternity rights at work. Enclose sae with your request.)

MAMA: Meet-a-Mum Association, 26a Cumnor Hill, Oxford OX2 9HA. Support and help for women suffering from postnatal depression.

National Childminding Association, 204-206 Bromley High Street, Bromley, Kent BR1 1PP. An organization to improve status and conditions of childminders, and standards of care for children.

Association of Breastfeeding Mothers, 131 Mayow Road, Sydenham, London SE26. 01-461 0022. 24-hour telephone service offering advice to breastfeeding mothers. Also local support groups.

4

Going Back To Work

A lot of women quite cheerfully give up work when they are expecting their first baby, and have only the vaguest possible notion of returning to their profession at some later date. Even in the 1980s, around 40 per cent of women do not have any paid employment outside the home.

All too many new mothers lapse into a kind of coma for four or five years, when their children are at the toddler stage, and achieve only domestic tasks.

At first, domestic life and freedom from office routine can seem like a welcome break from the hassle of daily commuting. There is no more jostling on dirty trains or crowded buses, no more short lunch breaks or difficult bosses. Instead, you are now the mistress in your own house, able to do exactly as you please.

But, all too often, the daily round can pall after a very few years, particularly when your children are no longer demanding all of your attention. You can always have another baby, of course, and the 'have another baby' syndrome is quite common in Western women, who can thus delay still further the time when decisions about personal developments have to be made.

But, at some time in their lives, an increasing number of women are starting to think: however am I going to get back to my job? You may have let membership of professional associations lapse long ago, and your contacts at work will almost certainly have moved on. At the very least, you can be sure that time will not have stood still in the working world. People several years younger than you will be in the job you left.

With gradually sinking heart, you can come to realize that all this childbearing and home management has not advanced your career one iota. In fact, the very reverse will have happened, and you will be seen as far less qualified than when you left your work.

One major reason, though by no means the only one, for so few women achieving significant success in careers is that they do not see their professional lives as a full time, unhindered commitment. This makes them tend to lack long term goals, and not have any clear idea of where they would like their career to lead them. Should you regard yourself primarily as a wage earner and worker, many women wonder, or mainly as a mother and home-maker?

I don't include the word 'wife' here, as I am sure the days when marriage was in itself regarded as a perfectly satisfactory career for a woman really have gone. But even highly motivated women are not always sure whether they should be career girls or mothers first, and wonder if in some way they have to 'choose', meaning that they will inevitably miss out on one aspect or the other.

There is also the inescapable fact – and a big factor that stops many women from returning to proper jobs – that paid work requires organization, and a certain amount of toughness, single-mindedness and self-confidence. Home, however boring, is at least a safe and known environment, whereas the working world can be a harsh jungle, where the natives are by no means always friendly. Any woman contemplating a return to work has to understand that she will be leaving a secure, unthreatening environment for an unknown one, where new and perhaps difficult challenges will have to be met.

This in itself can be frightening and is a reason why some women delay their return to work for ever-longer periods.

It is by no means uncommon for a woman to tell herself that she will go back when the youngest child is at playgroup. Then, when this day arrives, she tells herself that the time is not quite right, but that she will definitely go back when all the children are at infant school. Then, she decides she will go back when the children are at secondary school. Lastly, she feels it's better not to go back until they actually leave home. So she ends up never working again.

There is no law that says a woman, or a man for that matter, *has* to work, but it is most important to get one's ideas on the subject sorted out. The reasons for returning, or not returning, to work must be faced, so that there is not this endless see-sawing, with guilt feelings coming in to make life miserable all the time.

Suppose that you, for one reason or another, decided you would give up your work when your children were small, but now you would like to return. How easy or difficult is it?

It all depends on a great many factors, not least of which is your own attitude. You need to do a careful assessment of your personality, home commitments, and job opportunities in your area. Very many women move to executive-type estates, thinking this will be a nice environment for their children to grow up in, and then find themselves marooned there, with no public transport, no job opportunities, and no real escape. The men, meanwhile, are all thankfully on the 8.15 into the nearest big city.

Journalist Penny Perrick reckons it's not a bad idea, if you are at all career-minded, to bring kids up in the middle of the city. This makes it easier for you to work, and the kids won't have to be chauffeured everywhere. Some mothers spend several hours a day driving around, taking carloads of kids to school, Brownies, music lessons, swimming lessons, skating lessons, friends to tea, and the cinema.

Though the country may have many charms, it is not usually a good bet for the serious working woman. If you are contemplating a move to a leafier, more rural area, first investigate the job possibilities. If you are not a natural stay-at-homer, you won't be happy being stranded and isolated all day long.

Now, you have to ask yourself, why do you want to go back to work? Is it because you have become profoundly bored at home, because you want more status, or because you need more money? Or is it because you feel you have something unique to offer the job world, and feel you will remain unfulfilled in life otherwise? Are you missing your old job desperately, or do you hate being dependent on a man's income?

All these questions will require different answers, and will affect the type of job you eventually land. If money is an overwhelming factor, this could lead you to be more ambitious than might otherwise be the case. A need for status of your own can often fire enthusiasm as well, as can the desire for financial independence, whether or not you actually 'need' the money. But if you are just bored, you may not aim so high, and may remain content to take a series of low-paying, part-time jobs.

You would also have to work out whether you are now going to dedicate yourself to being a full-time career woman, or whether you only want to work, say, three days a week. If you are only half-hearted about work, your pay and career structure will tend to stay at a low level.

Women who have gained high professional qualifications and spend a number of years in full time work before 'retiring', will always find it far easier to slot back into work, at a similarly high level. There is always a desperate shortage of highly skilled, highly motivated people, in any profession, in spite of unemployment rates.

Those that possess skills which are in great demand will rarely find themselves out of work, as they will tend to be besieged with offers. But that is not the majority of people, and certainly not the majority of women.

If you intend to return to work at a professional level, you will need to look seriously at childcare options. Those who have been at home for several years, and whose children are past the infant stage, willl not need a trained nanny. A foreign au pair is probably the best answer here, and these girls are quite easy to recruit. They will, though, need a nice room of their own and plenty of time off to study.

School holidays are no problem, either, as there are always scores of older teenagers and students around who will be only too glad to look after your children in the daytime, and even stay overnight if necessary.

You may find it difficult at first having a stranger in the house but, on the whole, you won't be there when she is. Also, older children can positively benefit from having an au pair in the house, so long as she gets on with, and likes, the children. The atmosphere in the house can become more relaxed and international, less insular.

You may be offered a job out of the blue, as I once was. After going for interview, the boss asked if I could start the next day. I had no childcare fixed up at the time, as I was between jobs, but I said yes and, on arriving home, spent the rest of the day making frantic phone calls to friends, acquaintances and agencies. Needless to say, come 9 a.m. the next morning, a solution to the problem had been found. Those who are serious career women will take the job first, then worry about childminding arrangements later. These can always be solved, but jobs are not so easy to come by, particularly the exciting and interesting ones.

Really sizzling offers don't crop up very often, but it's always a good idea to accept them when they do. The family won't suffer. The older your children become, the less of a problem substitute childcare is. At any rate, if you are an average Western woman having two children, the very longest you could justify being out of the job market is 15 years. That still leaves at least 25 years – a quarter of a century – of working life. It is certainly worth obtaining the highest professional qualifications you can for those 25 years, and making sure you keep in touch, even if you are at home for some years.

Those who have not achieved professional qualifications will certainly find job hunting harder, especially if they are now, belatedly, after a satisfying and rewarding career. Specific advice for retraining for a second career is given in the next chapter, but if retraining is out of the question there is no need to despair. At the very least you could take a typing course at evening classes as these are ridiculously cheap, and offer yourself as a typist. It's not perhaps an interesting job in itself, but it can lead to other things.

Even cleaning need not be the dead-end job it at first seems. Celia and Brian Wright, who run the Green Farm Nutrition Centre, which sells vitamin supplements and offers courses in nutrition, now employ three of their former cleaning ladies as executives in their business. A return to work, however humble initially, can always open up other avenues in a way that staying at home never could. Even a little part-time job, which may be well below your capacities, helps with vital confidence rebuilding. It may help to try and do some work at home first, to see how you are able to discipline yourself to do it.

Slowly, an increasing number of courses are being planned to help women ease back into careers, to show them how to present themselves, offer samples of possible jobs, and give advice on interview techniques. There may be such a course available at your local further education college. It would be worth looking in your local library, as many of these courses are aimed at women who do not have obviously marketable skills. (one of these courses is described in more detail on page 96.)

Whatever you do decide, you must be prepared for a fairly tough time ahead. You are very likely to experience initial rejection, perhaps for the first time in many years – and there will inevitably be disappointments. You are unlikely to get the very first job you apply for, though this sometimes happen. Eddie Brennan was a housewife for seventeen years, then decided to apply for a job. In the event, she got the first job she sought and now, six years later, is on the board of directors of a firm exporting camera equipment.

She said: 'It wasn't long before I realized I wasn't quite as stupid as I had imagined. My skills hadn't atrophied as much as I thought they would, and I was soon able to bring myself up to date.' Eddie had trained in her native Australia as a bookkeeper, but had never worked in this country until eight years ago.

Another aspect of returning to work that can upset many women is the salaries that are on offer. Middle-aged women can be horrified at the lowness of the sums offered. In fact, low salaries are a bone of contention for many women, and can make them wonder whether returning to work is at all worth it. They may see their husbands, who themselves have never stopped work, earning handsome five-figure sums, and vaguely imagine that they are worth something similar. They can experience shock and disbelief, not unmingled with horror, when they learn that the most they can command is £6,000. This is, in 1985, still the average salary for women.

Unless they have very high-level skills, nobody is going to offer them £10,000 or £15,000, even if they are graduates with impressive work records behind them. Some women spend the years at home taking a further degree, and then discover that this does not fit them for any employment at all. A masters degree may show a fine knowledge of T. S. Eliot or seventeenth-century porcelain, but this is unlikely to land a decent-paying job.

There is absolutely no job in the world that pays high money for being able to do practically nothing. A long, uphill struggle will be called for, as you may have to persuade potential employers that you are worth taking on. They are not going to risk all that much on you at first, so you will have to prove yourself, and the longer you have been out of the job market, the harder this will be.

Women who are half-hearted about returning to work will be put off by the first hurdle they encounter and can use this as an excuse to scuttle back into the home. This is not, however, the stuff that readers of this book are made of.

A few years ago, a major workshop on the subject of women returning to work was held at the Westmoreland Hotel, London. It was presented by Margery Povall, of the City University, who has probably done more than any other female in this country to persuade employers to take the 'career break' into account. Her report makes interesting and enlightening, if salutary, reading. It reveals that, though many women might think they want to go back to work, in reality, they are not always prepared to give the necessary commitment.

While deploring the attitude that male employers often take, that women never come back after babies despite their protestations to the contrary, the report emphasizes that determination in the face of difficult odds is absolutely needed.

On the whole, nobody will be waiting out there with open arms to welcome you into a high-paying but easy job. Employers probably don't know you exist, and couldn't much care, until *you* persuade them that you are worth their serious consideration.

The report stated that only about five per cent of the nation's females are now working full time, if they have pre-school age children. While women now make up 42 per cent of the total labour force, two-fifths of these are concentrated in part-time jobs. About two-thirds of these are mothers, nearly all of whom are in low-paying positions. It is a depressing picture, but one which need not necessarily continue.

In a balanced world, there would be more women working in responsible posts. It's awful to think that our health, our taxation system, our legal system, our education, the church, and local government are all absolutely in the hands of one sex. The only way to make the world a fairer place for women, is for women themselves to be out there in the workplace, making their presence felt. A lot of highly qualified people are at the moment going to waste, and the 'maternal brain drain' is a very real problem. One writer to *The Guardian* recently said she could well understand why women weren't all that eager to return to work – who wants all that hassle and knives in the back, plus the fear of being made redundant, or getting the sack, she asked. Well, while we let the men have it all their own way and we just retreat into the home, this state of affairs will continue. A token woman may not be noticed but if half the executive workforce is female, that will certainly alter the company's profile.

Women tend to forsake their jobs when they are pregnant, partly because the maternity provisions may seem inadequate, partly because they often feel giving in their notice is expected of them, and partly because they genuinely feel their children will need them at home.

Some women may also feel it is almost impossible to do two jobs properly, and there is a definite reluctance to employ childminders or nannies. One reason why childcare facilities in this country are so notoriously poor is that all too many women still have the idea that it is wrong to leave their child and go out to work. In actual fact, the idea that a child should be holed up all day with just one adult is a very recent one. It plays no part in traditional societies, and has only been a feature of Western life for the past 50 years or so. In times gone by, aristocratic ladies hardly ever saw their children, and in peasant families, the kids received scant attention, as they were required to hoe the weeds or run errands almost as soon as they could walk. There is no evidence at all that children are in any way deprived by having a working mother. On the whole, I suspect, women are not holding down good jobs when they are mothers because they are not sure of what is right and proper for them to do.

One thing you can be sure of at home is that the competitive element, which looms so large in the working world, is absent. Of course, mothers compete with each other to see whose child talks first, or whose husband has the higher-paying job, but personal competition is not there. You can reign supreme in your own home, whereas at work you have to fit in with others. Far too few women are brought up to be part of a team. Even in games at school, girls tend to choose the individualistic sports rather than team games. Running your own show can seem far more attractive than being a cog in a mighty wheel, but of course, the drawbacks are many: no wages, no rewards, no promotion prospects, no appreciation.

Whenever you enter the marketplace, you will inevitably have to compete and be judged on performance. You risk being sacked, or being passed over, or being totally ignored. Some radical feminists feel this hierarchical system of the commercial world is wrong, and should be replaced by a more co-operative attitude.

But again, that won't happen until women start to have a significant voice in the marketplace. Then, they can make sure things happen their way.

Because so very many women lack a positive attitude to the hierarchy of the working world, they tend not to plan ahead, but drift along hoping, like Mr Micawber, that something will turn up. Margery Povall said: 'One big problem is that women don't plan enough in their careers.

Childcare alone cannot be a sufficient reason for half the population to be financially dependent on the other half, either personally or through state benefits.'

It may be impossible for you to go straight back to a job, either because it is so long since you worked, and have forgotten how to apply for jobs, or conduct yourself at an interview, or because you don't imagine there is any earning work that you could do. Certainly, your confidence is likely to be at a very low ebb after several years at home.

The needs of women in this position are just beginning to be realized, and there are now courses you can attend which are designed specifically to ease your passage back into the working world. One such pioneer programme was arranged in 1981 by the Brooklands School of · Management in Weybridge, which runs Career Development Courses for both men and women. This particular course, lasting for six weeks, was organized under the auspices of Wider Opportunities for Women, part of the Training Opportunities Scheme (TOPS). It was a free course, lasting for six weeks, non-residential, and was heavily advertised through posters and leaflets. You even got paid for attending – about £40 a week.

The course included job sampling, visits to companies, help with writing CVs, and identifying specific career problems. Its function was to act as a 'bridge' whereby women could assess the practical consequences of returning to work. Twelve women signed up for this course, ranging in formal qualifications from solicitor to cook and nursery nurse. None of the women had worked recently, and one or two had not been in paid employment for 20 years or more. Ages ranged from 30 to 50 plus. The women were all asked why they wanted to go back to work, and financial considerations were hardly a factor for most of them. The objectives of the course were: to explore the domestic and other problems in returning to work, and offer some solutions; to make participants aware of the cons, as well as the pros, of paid employment; to advise them on expectations of employers, and to help them present themselves effectively. The whole course sounded like a wonderful opportunity but it was not, as it turned out, overwhelmingly popular. It did, though, enable some common problems facing women returners to be sorted out; and one of the most striking was a general lack of confidence. It is well known now that redundant executives lose confidence in their ability to find another job after six months, so how much greater is this when you may not have worked for many years. The outside world can seem a truly frightening and hostile place.

People who have spent several months confined to the home, or in hospital, can often feel nervous about going out and getting on a bus.

Confidence is, for most people, a very fragile and easily-lost commodity, but it must return before you can ever hope to make a success of going back to work. My sister-in-law, who was a competent and lively reporter on a provincial newspaper for many years, left to start a family. When, three years later, she began to pick up the threads of her former job, which she had been able to do almost with her eyes shut, she found an inexplicable nervousness about phoning up her former contacts. She said: 'It's amazing. I've known all these people as friends for years. I was even nervous about filing a story, something I had been doing every day for almost 10 years.'

Jenny found, though, that after a very short time, her anxiety disappeared, and she was back in the swing again. But even she, who has been of an independent spirit since early teenagerhood, and had kept in touch all the time with home-based freelance work, found that returning took a surprising amount of 'oomph'.

Some women who attended the pioneer returners course at Brooklands felt that they couldn't even hold down a minor part-time job. The tutors also noticed a definite tendency to be easily discouraged, another problem that bedevils many women from childhood on, and not just those trying to go back to work. The course tutors noted, in addition, a lack of initiative and self-discipline. This may have stemmed from years of dependency in the home, of 'learned helplessness'. Whilst understandable, these negative tendencies will militate against your finding your feet once more in the outside world. Some of the women on the course became easily distracted and tended to postpone awkward tasks, such as phoning for an appointment for job sampling. The tutors discovered, however, that initiatives improved with time so, again, it all boils down to confidence.

One of the prerequisites of being a successful employee is to be punctual. When I met Eddie Brennan's boss at a party, he said: 'The thing about Eddie is that she is never even a minute late.' On the controversial Exegesis courses, which are supposed to make you instantly successful in the business world, they turn you out if you are a minute late because, to them, lack of punctuality indicates lack of commitment. Their view is that, if you are late, you *meant* to be late.

The Brooklands tutors found that the participants tended to blame domestic matters for arriving late and leaving early. This is something that may be tolerated on a free course, but will not be countenanced at work.

Those contemplating a return to work may worry that their knowledge and skills are now out of date. But according to Margery Povall, this is a problem often more in the mind than a reality. If you have a basic structure of skills that go with a particular job, you can pick up new techniques and knowledge in a very short time indeed. There are hardly any jobs, she said, where knowledge would go impossibly out of date, even after a gap of 10 years or more.

The idea that skills can go out of date instantly is often used as an excuse not to go back to work. I have even heard former primary school teachers, who have not worked for many years, excuse their continuing absence from the classroom by saying they would now be too out of date. But children are the same from generation to generation: how can you be out of date? In high tech jobs, it's different of course but, even here, you can catch up very quickly, if you have a mind to.

An increasing number of professions are now offering refresher or 'rustproofing' courses, for women to bring their skills up to date before applying for jobs. So, definite attempts are being made to reinclude women in the workforce, even if these are rather sporadic as yet. If you want information on refresher courses, contact your professional association, who will let you know whether these are available in your area.

Another problem encountered on the Brooklands course was that some of the participants were attracted to the course itself, and did not seriously intend to get a job. There is a trend among middle-class women, particularly, to become 'course groupies' and go from one to another, rather than ever settling down into a proper work pattern. There is nothing wrong with going on courses in theory, except that it underlines the impression many employers are getting, that so many women are just not serious about going back to work.

Hopping from one course to another does offer short-term solutions, but you are liable to feel as empty at the end as you did at the beginning, unless you are doing it for a specific purpose.

The Brooklands course was the first of its kind and as such was, perhaps, not perfect. But it does illustrate some points that any woman wishing to return to work should consider: the first is that, the longer you leave it, the more difficult a return will be and, second, women who are contemplating spending several years at home should be aware that, unless they make efforts to keep in touch with their previous profession, they may find the years spent at home are completely lost as far as career advancement is concerned.

Ken Hyett, organizer of the Career Development Courses at Brooklands, where five WOW courses have now been completed, said: 'Many women are surprised when they realize that it is not that easy to return to work, and that major adjustments may have to be made, both to their lifestyle and their attitudes.'

Clearly, a return is easier in the recognized professions. Career breaks can now be managed quite well, for women who have gained impressive professional qualifications and put in several years' work experience before leaving for domestic reasons. As yet, there is no concerted, nationwide, 'career break' scheme which will enable women to combine job and family satisfactorily. But the need has now been recognized, and the paragraphs following will give an idea of how some professions are tackling the situation.

It now needs an almighty push from the women themselves to (a) persuade the relevant professions to provide seminars and weekends to keep skills up to date and (b) for more flexibility in working hours. There is, in fact, no God-given reason why everybody has to work from nine to five. But these hours have, in the past, suited a mainly male workforce, who have people at home to see to their domestic needs.

There is a big move on at the moment to attract more women into engineering, but the fact of the matter is that, as yet, few women engineers ever do return to their previous jobs after having a family. Yet, for those so inclined, the time spent at home can now be used to keep in touch with new developments. There are now Open University Associate Student Courses designed specially for women in this position. So if you are serious about going back to work in an engineering-based job, you can apply to the OU for details. The courses are not expensive, and would enable you to keep your skills up to date. Also, if you might want to return, never completely lose touch with your old firm, or your professional association. They may ask you to come in for relief or casual work, and it helps a return to full-time work later, if you are able to show work experience while basically being at home.

The Third Hand is a Bristol-based organization for part-time social workers. It is aimed at those women who have taken a career break, but who want to stay in touch to return full-time later. Refresher and 'rustproofing' courses are held regularly, and part-time opportunities continuously scanned and scrutinized. An appointments register is also kept, as many women, both in social work and other professions, feel they would rather work their way back gradually than take a full-time job straightaway. Some enlightened employers, not just in social work, will have highly qualified women back on a part-time basis, and this is a very good way of staying in touch.

Banking is a profession that employs very many women, but nearly all are in the very lowest grades. Even today, only one per cent of managerial posts are held by women. In 1981, however, the National Westminster Bank designed a re-entry package for women who are absolutely serious about wanting to return to a proper career with good promotion prospects, rather than just a job.

The commitment before full-time return is not large: only two weeks' relief work a year, but this must be kept. The long-term aim of this scheme is to attract more bright women into banking, and in some cases, re-entry at a career grade can now be guaranteed. Other large firms are now looking into re-entry programmes. These include the GLC and the Civil Service. Nowadays, in the Civil Service, you can apply for a job at your former grade for a period of three years after leaving to have a baby. Maternity provisions in this profession are also very generous, as you are allowed up to a year, including both paid and unpaid leave, to return to your former job.

There are also several schemes on offer for women doctors to return to work, or to continue their training on a part-time basis, while their children are small.

Margery Povall gives this advice for women who are considering a return to work: 'Try to build up expectations of returning to the same place you left. This is not a popular piece of advice, as many women leave work with a huge sigh of relief. But it is a fact that it is far easier to return to a work place where you are known, than one where you have no contacts whatsoever.

'Before you actually do leave, talk about returning, even if you feel this is unlikely at the time. Then you become known as a person who is still interested, and you may be asked to take on occasional relief work. Do this if you can, as it will be a definite help when you want to return on a more permanent basis.'

You should also use all the friends you have to make contacts, and establish a wide network of possible job leads. Many women are reluctant to mix up friendships and work contacts, unlike men, but it must be done. If the only people you know are friends, rather than work mates, as it is so long since you worked, use these to obtain advice.

Keep in touch with someone who is already in the sort of work you would like if you can. It's all a question of keeping in close contact with the world of work, and following any job leads that sound promising.

Try to form a realistic impression of the work you can do, and what you would be able to offer. Many people consider only what they can take, but you have a far better chance of obtaining interesting work if you think instead about what you are able to give. Women often have a very low impression of themselves, and imagine they are worth hardly anything to anybody. It can be this fear that stops them applying for jobs in the first place.

Do read all the career counselling books you can lay your hands on, and go through them in a systematic way, to discover what your skills are, and how they would fit in.

If you left your last place of employment with a huge sigh of relief you may not relish returning to it. But you may still be able to work in the same field. Perhaps you were a nurse, and don't like the thought of going back to work in a hospital. But you can still choose from a wide variety of jobs, if you have had nursing experience. You may not like the idea of wearing a white cap and emptying bedpans, but you may consider private nursing, helping out at a health centre, or working in a favourite charity, even in a voluntary capacity, perhaps, at first. You may like to work in an old people's or children's home. The time spent at home could help you to clarify your idea of what you really like doing. You may prefer to visit people in their homes, rather than working in an institution. The health area is a large and expanding one, particularly in the 'alternative' fields. Very many ex-nurses are now using their skills to help cancer patients, or handicapped children.

Maybe you were a teacher, but the thought of going back to school, and coping with school meals, other staff and hundreds of kids all day long, gives you the heeby jeebies. But you can still use your teaching skills, in less obvious ways. There is a very large field of adult education, from basic literacy to O-level classes. If you have maths qualifications, you can take pupils in your home – no need to worry about a shortage of work!

It is less easy to secure teaching jobs than used to be the case, but anybody with a science qualification should have little difficulty in finding work. As with medicine, the field of education is a large one. You may like to drive round to the homes of children who need home tuition because they are ill, or handicapped. Most local authorities have such schemes going.

Don't imagine that, because you weren't high-powered in the job you left, that the world of satisfying work is now forever closed to you. Very many women only really wake up, workwise, after they have had children, and discover for themselves that the domestic life need not be all in all. Very often, when women leave to have children, they imagine that now they will be leading their 'proper' role in life, and live happily ever after. When girls are questioned about their future plans, they hardly ever see much beyond the age of 30 for themselves. But, having reached this age, they realize there's an awful lot of life left.

But the reality is hardly like the romantic dream, and even if you don't divorce, you may want to do something individual with your life later. The important thing is not to leave it too late, if you can help it. Though 40 is only halfway through an average life, few employers want to take on a 40-year-old trainee.

The whole thing can become very depressing if you keep postponing the day when you will do something about returning to work. But before returning, it is vital that you view work as of importance in your life.

Even today, it is undeniable that there is still a class element in returning to work, and a distinction is made between women who 'have' to work, and those who 'choose' to. There is still some status in being able to say: 'I don't have to work for the money.' Women whose financial contribution is seen as being essential to the tiny family budget are to be pitied, rather than admired by society at large. Those women who do not have to return to work in order to keep body and soul together have a more cavalier and dilettante attitude about the work they do.

Also, for middle-class women with high-earning husbands, it may not be very enhancing for his reputation if you are able to secure only a low-level job. So for women whose husbands have moved to near the top of the earning ladder, it can be better to remain a potential worker for ever, and someone who gave up a 'promising' career. It may be easier never actually to try, than to risk rejection, and being offered derisory pay.

But it is here, thinks Margery Povall, that the WOW courses can be so supportive. They offer a network whereby you can keep in touch with the other women on the course and compare experience. It is always easier to have friends and acquaintances in the same boat, as you can feel so alone and helpless when trying to get a job, and forever appearing to fail. If you keep in touch with other people on the course, you can comfort each other when rejections occur, as they are very likely to. A support group can be invaluable when, at last, you pluck up courage to apply for a job, and find you don't get it. Women trying to return can need reassurance that they are not unemployable good-for-nothings, when they don't find it easy to get themselves a job.

A career break can always be managed when you have kept in touch. It is when women want to assume their careers after many, many years of not bothering about them that serious difficulties can arise.

Here, if you have lost touch completely with your former place of work, you could try to recover contacts by telephoning those you once worked with, even if it was several years ago. That could help to establish a network whereby, gradually, contacts are made with those who are presently there. This will be harder if you have moved to another part of the country, and may, of course, be altogether impossible if you are now living in a different part of the world.

Should renewing former contacts prove too daunting a task, you may be able to get in touch with a firm similar to the one you worked for before you left paid employment. It does take quite a lot of courage to ring people up out of the blue, but once you've made up your mind to do it, the task becomes less nerve-racking than you might imagine. Whenever you are afraid, just *do* it, and don't think too much about the fear. Once you have made a few difficult phone calls, you will find that the nervousness vanishes.

When you have managed to track down some people who are, or were, in the same line of work as yourself, you can ask if they know of any vacancies, or whom you might contact. It's surprising how soon you can get a line of job leads and, sooner or later, these will lead to a job in actuality.

Having said this, never actually rely on friends to get you jobs, as they are obviously less interested in finding you work than you are in getting it. The hard effort, initiative and impetus must always come from you. The desired job may not materialize immediately but, if pursued with vigour, you are bound to be successful before long. Don't, though, become an instant nuisance, ringing people up at inconvenient times, and demanding that they speak to you. It is possible to appear over-aggressive, simply through nervousness.

But you should not miss any opportunity to let the word go round that you are now looking for work, and are eligible for certain posts that may crop up. It is useful to remember that, wherever you go, you should keep on the lookout – at dinner parties, children's parties, coffee mornings, on holiday – you never know just when that right contact will come into your life. And it is an indisputable fact of life that, when you are sending out strong signals that you are looking for work, before long an offer will come. Everything you do starts from that determined thought.

Those who are vague, wishy-washy or ambivalent in their intentions to return to work, will find that offers never come, and that the right jobs always seem to go to somebody else. This happens when you are not giving the matter enough concerted attention.

In this chapter, we have been assuming that you will want to return to the job or profession you trained for but have now left. If you have not kept in touch with your work at all, you may need to reassess your qualifications. This can include informal ones, as well as pieces of paper. It is true that homemaking and childbearing are seen as detracting from, rather than adding to, a professional life, but you may not exactly have been idle over the non-employed years.

If you have done any public speaking, however minor, or sat on committees, such as Parent Teacher Associations, add these into your CV. Also put down work done for any local environmental or conservation groups, as well as involvement in local politics. Helping out at the Citizens' Advice Bureau, or marriage guidance work, aiding mentally handicapped children or delivering Meals on Wheels, can all become important 'qualifications' when you are looking for paid work. They add up to a total impression of you as a person, so never dismiss voluntary work, hobbies done to a high standard, or community involvement.

On the other hand, if you *haven't* done work of this kind, don't try and make out you have. It never pays to tell outright lies when applying for jobs. Some people imagine they can put down false positions, or salaries, as it was all a long time ago. But these things can be checked, and they often are.

You may also have amassed some valuable skills over the non-working years, by going to evening classes, or becoming incredibly proficient at interior decorating. Maybe you have taken a French or German course, helped your husband with his accounts, or learned to type and take shorthand. Perhaps you have been on a computer literacy course. Also, any formal courses you have taken, such as an Open University Degree, a personal effectiveness course, or Cordon Bleu cookery diploma, should go down. Never leave out any achievements, even if they do seem very 'housewifely'.

When contemplating a return, think back to the jobs you have most enjoyed doing while at home. Do you actively like planning holidays, or arranging complicated menus? Are you a natural hostess, with a talent for making people feel at ease? Are you good at standing up for your rights? Are you, perhaps, extremely neat and methodical, liking to have everything in order? Thinking hard about all these aspects will help you to decide exactly which kind of job you would like to go after.

You will also have to think carefully about the amount of time you are prepared to give to a job. Would you be willing to take a full-time post, and also study for further qualifications? Could you travel at all? Could you accept work that might take you to other countries from time to time? However remote the possibility seems, do consider all these variables, as you never know when they might crop up.

Elizabeth Dobbie, of the National Advisory Centre on Careers for Women, gives the following advice in her handbook *Returners*: start by going to your local job centre – you can do this even if you are not seriously looking for work, and see which kind of jobs are on offer, and just what kind of salaries they are paying. Also note the qualifications and experience asked for, with any job that interests you. Could you afford to travel to and from work, buy extra clothes, get domestic help and still be in pocket from your job? If not, you may have to reconsider your first thought.

Job sharing

This is a distinct possibility for the woman who is completely serious about work, but who wants to give time to the family as well. Job sharing is quite a new idea, and is not at all like part-time work. It implies a genuine commitment to the job, and involves sick pay, promotion prospects and pension schemes. It works exactly like a full-time job, except that two people do it. Normally, such jobs are completely split down the middle, and your sharer would need to bring to the job a commitment exactly equal to yours. Most people who embark on successful job sharing schemes find that it is essential to have a good relationship with the sharer, and to have communication outside work hours.

A few years ago, most employers looked very askance at employers who asked to share a job, as to them it looked very like laziness. But now job sharing operates in many parts of the country, and is rapidly becoming a valid alternative to the conventional work pattern.

To share a job well, you need to liaise with somebody whose attitude and seniority level would be similar to your own. It is best to get together and work it all out, before approaching a prospective employer with a job sharing proposal. Such schemes already operate in several professions, including teaching, banking, social work, the probation service, local government, medicine, and charity work. When a husband and wife are in identical professions, it may make sense for them to share their job, and this is already happening in some cases. It is an idea which could certainly grow over the next few years.

It means that both halves of the couple have an equal commitment to both their work and to the family. To me, job sharing between husband and wife is one of the most egalitarian ways of conducting a modern relationship. I have met several husband and wife social workers who feel this is an ideal solution. Granted, your income is halved, but then you would not have to spend on childminding or, as a woman, lose valuable years out of your career. One couple I know, who are both sub-editors on a national newspaper, have recently persuaded their company to let them operate a job-sharing scheme. As they are in identical jobs, earning identical salaries, it seemed like a sensible idea. It has also enabled them to give up their nanny, and release her room for a lodger so, money-wise, they are about as well off as before.

One example of a successful job sharing scheme is quoted below. You don't have to have spent years looking after a family to have considered this option, and it makes sense to get the arrangement a reality before you actually leave to have a baby.

Probation workers Penny Neale and Sarah Kershaw started sharing their job in 1982. They were both with the Inner London Probation Service, and were the first people in their profession to try the experiment. 'It has worked wonderfully well with us,' said Sarah, 'and it could be extended to many more professions.'

This is the way it was worked out for Penny and Sarah: they are both in the same GLC pension scheme, and retain all their rights and obligations as employees. They also receive yearly increments, and half the full car allowance. Their holiday entitlements are also split down the middle.

The day-to-day working out of the timetable was left to them, but they discovered it worked out best to do half a day each, and let the sharer take over at lunchtime. Their belief is that, for the scheme to work properly, both sharers must be in harmony with the other's ideas. There has to be a feeling of mutual trust, otherwise delicate situations such as might occur in probation work, could be worsened, rather than improved.

Penny Neale, who was in probation work for 10 years before deciding to share, says: 'The important thing is that we are in tune with each other. We each live about five minutes' distance from each other, and are on the phone constantly to sort out problems. We leave messages in the office as well.

'But I wouldn't say the job share has increased the total amount of paperwork. It all worked out beautifully, and we have been getting a lot of interest from other probation officers, in different parts of the country.'

As theirs was the first such scheme in this country among probation workers, the two women were monitored constantly for two years. Penny chose to share because she wanted to develop other interests, and Sarah was having her first baby. She said: 'I knew I wanted to continue work after the baby, but wasn't sure whether I would be able to manage a full-time job. This seemed to be the ideal arrangement.'

In job sharing schemes, if one person leaves, the solution is that half the job would then be advertised. It is not, sharers themselves emphasize, for women (or men) who simply want to pick up some pin money. It must be regarded as seriously as full-time work, and as a career, not just a little part-time interest.

Careers that can stand a break
In many career books written for women, you find that the 'career break' is now assumed to be almost an automatic happening. In most cases, women still take time out from a career when they have a family, but this is not always the only reason. There may be other considerations

for wanting to take a short break, such as writing a book, suddenly having to look after an aged relative, or wanting to go round the world. It is worth knowing exactly which careers can take a break, should you be comtemplating one for any reason. There are many jobs where a return would be difficult, if not impossible.

A full list of careers which welcome returners is given in Ruth Miller's *Equal Opportunities* Careers Guide, but here is a short list, to give an idea of those professions where a break is possible. *Accounting:* those who are members of professional bodies can keep in touch via journals and lectures, and this is very strongly advised. There is always a demand for accountants of either sex, and part-time work should be fairly easily available. This is an expanding profession, and as yet there are far too few women accountants. It is, though, a very good job for women to consider, as there is so much variety and flexibility within the profession. You can run your own small practice, work part-time for a local firm, or be chief accountant in a huge multinational organization.

You would probably find it extremely difficult, if not altogether impossible, to return to the world of *advertising*. Young, bright graduates are preferred here, and this profession is quick-changing, highly competitive and aggressive. Anybody who took a break would not find it very easy to get back. So if this is your job, hang on to it. Part-time and freelance are not easy within advertising, either.

Architects can return only if they have methodically kept up through journals and attending lectures and seminars. You have to make a conscious effort, and it may not be easy when you are surrounded by babies, nappies and washing.

Broadcasting: This can be a very flexible job, and very many women do return after a break, sometimes of considerable length. Notable examples are Jean Metcalfe and Mavis Nicholson. It is also possible to break into broadcasting at a later age, but you would have to be knowledgeable about some area of interest.

In the *Civil Service*, a return is now possible, and you can be considered for executive grades up to the age of 45. It used to be 28, until a test case changed the regulations.

In *engineering*, women are very welcome indeed to return to their previous employment, and in fact firms are now falling over backwards to encourage them to do just this.

Hairdressing: no problem, as you can always keep up by doing people's hair at home.

Journalism: Few women who have broken into this fascinating but highly competitive career ever want to leave it, so breaks are unlikely.

But, so is returning. You would have had to reach a very high position first, as most publications feel that young blood is to be preferred, except in the executive posts. It would be virtually impossible to train as a journalist in later life, as you would have to persuade a paper to take you on, and they are keener on young recruits.

Law: There is no real problem here, so long as you are relatively established before taking a break, and make a determined effort to spend the away time keeping up with changes in the law. An up-to-date approach is always impressive to prospective employers.

Librarian: no difficulties with career breaks, as this profession is not subject to rapid changes.

Medicine: this is possible, but only if you have kept up, or continued your training part-time. It would not be easy for a woman doctor who has spent, say, ten years completely away from the profession, to return.

It is extremely easy to return to *nursing*, as there are many hospitals, charities and institutions crying out for mature, sympathetic, qualified nurses. And there are always plenty of ill people around.

All *therapists*, whether speech, occupational or physio, can easily return, and there is constantly a demand for good people in these professions.

Personnel work: yes, if you have kept up in the usual way. There are, at the time of writing, no specific refresher courses available for would-be returners to personnel work.

The Police force: returners are usually considered only up to the age of 30, but it becomes easier the higher up you were when you left.

In *radiography*, a return is possible, but you may well have to do some retraining as this profession is quickly changing.

Secretarial work is easy enough for those who qualified as proper secretaries, but may be difficult for those who rose only to office junior or typists. 'Ageism' prevails in this job, and few employers relish the prospect of employing unskilled older ladies.

In *the Armed Services*, a return is rarely possible, though there is actually nothing against it in theory. It's just that, in practice, you must be prepared to move around.

Social work: returners are positively welcome, as maturity is a definite asset in this career.

Teaching: yes, again, returners are also encouraged, though you may feel you need to take a short retraining course first. Details are available on this from the Department of Education and Science.

If you intend to return to teaching, you may qualify for a retraining grant. It is well worth making enquiries, if you are worried about being rusty on your teaching skills.

It is a fact that the more you enjoy your career, the less happy you will be to relinquish it. There is a definite excitement that comes from pursuing a satisfying career, and it is something that even the most wonderful husband and beautiful children can never compensate for. Much female depression comes, I believe, from women at home pining for their lost careers. They can miss the wage packet, the camaraderie, the feeling that they were part of a unit, even though this may not consciously be realized. Numerous studies on the subject have shown that women who embark on a rewarding career are less likely to suffer from minor aches and pains, or even major illnesses, than stay-at-home females.

We have by no means completely solved the problem of women and work, and the whole question of returning becomes more problematic when you gratefully left a job you hated. To return to *that*, you may ask? Not likely! Margery Povall has noticed, in her researches, that many modern women still feel they must get married, set up home and have a family, all as soon as possible. For these women, a paying job may be seen purely as a way of providing the three-piece suite, the down-payment on a home, or for some other extremely domestic use, rather than being in any way fulfilling in its own right.

Some disgruntled feminists point out – and rightly – that 90 per cent of women's jobs, the paid as well as the unpaid ones, are dreary, badly paid and low in status. That may be so, but the only way to improve your status is to carry on working, and try to get better jobs, rather than opting out completely. If you opted out of a monotonous, low-paying job years before, you can hardly expect to return straight to an exotic job paying £20,000 a year. But, very often, those women who rushed so headlong into home, family and domestic commitments – what novelist and playwright John Mortimer has called the mighty rush into middle-age – later feel they have completely missed out, and then they wonder about going back to work.

These women, stuck at home without qualifications or experience, read about other women doing exciting, independent things, and earning lots of money. They then start to wonder whether life has utterly passed them by. This realization may dawn when the children are teenagers, by which time the premature mother will still only be in her mid-thirties, and have about 50 years of life in front of her.

Unless you can spend years training – and this will be considered in all its implications in the following chapter – you can only expect to return to a fairly low-level job. On the whole, women returners come back anyway to a lower level job than the one they left, and this goes for the higher reaches, as well as the bottom ones. A deputy headmistress who has left to have a baby will probably have to return to her profession as an ordinary teacher and then work her way back up. But if you haven't even qualified as anything, don't despair and reach for the tranquillizers to blot out each boring day. There are now opportunities for women in this position, and WOW and similar courses could well be the spur you need to get you back to thinking about work. Don't forget, too, that you get paid for going on them.

It takes people different lengths of time to 'find themselves', and women may take far longer than men because of the ambivalence they often feel about their own futures. Do keep in mind though, that the years spent childminding and homekeeping will have taught you valuable lessons about yourself, that may not have been apparent when you were a working girl.

You have very probably discovered skills you never knew you had, such as for gardening, cooking, dressmaking, or balancing budgets. All of these can eventually be turned to commercial advantage, given the will and determination. Perhaps you can become a school cook, or go to work in a garden centre. Use the skills you have gained since leaving work, and be aware that they are definite assets just as much as 100 wpm in shorthand.

Two other types of returners have yet to be considered, and both are perhaps of the more reluctant type. One is the worker who has suddenly been made redundant, and sees no possibility of being able to return to the same type of work. Redundancy constitutes one of the big shocks of life today, and it may take several months to recover from an unexpected blow. Your best bet here is to find a local self-help group, which counsels people on how to cope with redundancy, and then, before apathy sets in, start job seeking in earnest. I feel that, for anybody suddenly made redundant, it is better to take a job, any job, than to sit around doing nothing and mooching. A job can lead to another job, and other opportunities will soon open up.

Whatever you do, if you are redundant, think very carefully about spending any redundancy money on lavish courses organized for the newly unemployed. These can cost several hundred pounds, and leave you as jobless as before. If you have some money to spend, use it on booking up a course that will lead directly to employable skills. TOPS courses are organized for people in just your position, so do use them.

The other type of reluctant returner is the wife who never expected to have to work – until suddenly her husband upped and left her or, perhaps, she was left unexpectedly a widow. Either way, she is a woman who has now lost the financial support she expected to have throughout her life, and who now has to fend for herself. This may come after years of dependency as a wife.

How is such a woman to pave a way through the working jungle? A letter written to *The Times* from just such a woman illustrates the problems:

After being given the conjugal sack, the second stark truth to hit a woman left to fend for herself is that, when there wasn't quite enough money beforehand, half the insufficiency is very little indeed.

So it is a question of girding up the loins and finding work, which is where the third stark truth comes home. Getting back isn't easy. Plans for the gradual return to full-time work as the children grew older, carefully laid with the long-term future in mind, fly out of the window. A job is needed now, urgently, before you drown in the sea of unpaid bills . . .

You pluck up courage to ring old contacts to find that they have retired, died or moved on. You don't fit in: too highly qualified to be taken on as a trainee, too rusty to be considered at the level your qualifications on paper would justify. You are passed around people like an embarrassing parcel. You are told to keep quiet about that Master's degree you slaved over for so long and were so proud of, because 'you don't want to seem too clever, dear.' The refrain is: 'Can you type? Can you type? Can you type?' Getting divorced is bad enough, but somehow becoming a typist seems the last straw.

Experience! Doesn't bringing up children count for anything, coping with birth and death, frantically fitting in essays and revising for exams while making birthday cakes in the shape of Winnie the Pooh and getting the mud out of rugby shirts?

What one wants, of course, is a nice little rung at the bottom of a very long ladder, where the shattered ego can rest in routine and subordination, and then, as healing progresses, work gradually to a position of fulfilment. Getting back is like praying for snow in the Sahara.

It is always simplicity itself, of course, to solve other people's problems, as one hasn't oneself got the emotional involvement in the situation. But first, I would say to the writer of this letter (after all, there are plenty of women in just this situation these days): what sort of work are you expecting to get? Do you see yourself working for a small firm, or large company and if so, in what capacity? What exactly can you do? If you can't type, can you edit, proofread, book-keep, do accounts, handle tax problems, counsel people, buy clothes for a large store, order in supplies from abroad, teach French or maths? It's no use saying you can work quickly and accurately under pressure. The question is: what at?

As a journalist, I can work quickly and, I hope, accurately, under pressure if I'm writing a story on which I have enough information, but I couldn't repair a car quickly and accurately, under pressure or not. Also, would the writer of this letter fit in with colleagues in an office? Is she chatty and extrovert, or shy and restrained? Could she be a librarian?

Of course, you are not going to be able to get a job unless you know specifically what areas you want to aim at. A woman who has not worked outside the house for many years will have to prove her worth. She cannot suddenly go from earning nothing to earning a five-figure salary unless she has some extremely saleable skills. Most people in high-earning jobs have got there gradually, with annual increments and promotions. Unless you have acquired these, you are bound to have to start again at the bottom, even though jobs there are low in status and low in pay.

If you have only five years' work experience in total, this is what you will be paid for, regardless of how old you are, or how many degrees you may have accumulated in the meantime. Anybody can swot for an exam, but it takes different qualities to work in a highly-organized and structured office.

Divorced and separated women can be extremely reluctant about having to go out and work at all, as the writer of the letter to *The Times* was. She did, theoretically at least, intend to go back to work at some stage but, like St Augustine when he prayed for chastity, not yet, O Lord.

The attitude of this writer will actually stop her from landing a good job. If she were less resentful about having to go out to work, and more positive about what she had to offer a wage-paying employer, she would find job hunting far more fruitful. Nobody wants a reluctant worker.

But if you find, to your cost, that there is nothing employable you can do, even though you may be a graduate with a double first and a PhD, there are worse solutions than learning to type. The Sight and Sound course takes only a few weeks and, at the end of it, at least you will have a saleable skill, and it gives you a starting point. Once in, you can show your employers that you are worthy of more than the typing pool or addressing envelopes, and can progress.

Like Eddie Brennan, whose story was briefly related earlier, if you show you can do the job, you will soon gain promotion.

It is the case that more and more women are being forced into the position of earning a wage. In America, there is even an organization, called Displaced Homemakers, that caters for women like this.

There is, inevitably, always a great deal of trauma accompanying a divorce or separation, as your whole way of life comes crashing about your ears, and carefully-laid plans go bust in an instant. Women going through a divorce can be in such a state of shock that getting back to work is made even more difficult. If you can, it would be better to wait until you are in a calmer state of mind before even looking for a job, as employers can sense desperation, and don't like it.

Nobody is going to give you a job out of charity, but will employ you only if they think you are the woman for the job, whatever your domestic circumstances may be.

If you want to re-enter the world as a working woman, a WOW course could well be the best initial step. An assertiveness training course could also stand you in good stead, as could joining a divorced and separated person's club. Some of these exist to match you up again, but a careful assessment beforehand should ensure you don't join the wrong type.

Divorced women looking for a job should avoid all self-pity and the 'poor little me' attitude. Most divorced couples do find there is simply not enough money to go round, however generous the ex-husband might wish to be. There is also now a definite move to make women without dependent children self-supporting after divorce. So nobody can assume these days, that there will always be a man around to provide. The worst aspect to strike many divorced women is that they are aware they have now lost their status, and their standard of living, if they have been living through their husbands.

Bitterness can be long-lasting unless you make a conscious effort to drive bitter feelings out and realize that these can only ever drag you down, not lift you up. But, of the divorced women I have met, many have felt that the whole business, though nasty in the extreme, did enable them to discover who they were, and to get back into the working world. They re-identified themselves as proper people, as individuals in their own right.

Those who have been used to a high standard of living, courtesy of their husband's salary, may have to get used to the fact that they cannot command anything like what he has been earning. They may consider themselves their ex's equal, but employers probably won't see it that way. Often, humble pie has to be eaten, but rapid strides can be made once the first foot in the door has been established.

The beauty of a WOW course is that it will confront you with all these hard realities at the outset, so that sinking feeling never has a chance to set in. It often happens that one gains an unrealistic view of the outside world, and what you could be earning, when you are actually sitting at home earning nothing.

Ideally, your family life should be enhanced rather than disrupted by your return to work. If you are married, it is a good idea to discuss the proposed return with your husband at every stage, and enlist his support. I say, here, support and not permission, as a grown woman should not need her husband's permission to go out to work.

Wives often complain that they do not get co-operation, and that their husbands are actively opposed to their working. It may be that some antediluvian males take this attitude but, in my experience, they are far from being in the majority. Most actually prefer their wives to work, as it adds to, rather than takes away from, their 'masculine' status. A man who can attract a high-flying career woman, rather than a dependent grown-up child, is envied, not pitied. This reminds me of the time I was at a conference, talking to a group of female freelance colleagues. One man was there.

He said, eventually: 'I wish I had a pretty wife who went out to work and earned lots of money.' The witty rejoinder from one of my female colleagues was: 'Yes, that's what we'd all like!'

Of course, it may be an initial shock to the family not to have you there all the time, seeing to their meals and clean clothes, but most men don't really notice these things. If they do notice, they don't much care – it's the women who are bothered about being 'home to get John's supper'.

Before actually returning to work, you may need to re-educate your family into fending for themselves a little more round the house. If you have let yourself slide imperceptibly into a servant role, they may be taking you quite for granted. Let them see you are not a servant, and that food and clothes don't appear by magic. You will now need help with shopping, washing up and housework, and they can lend a hand. But you will very likely find that the amount of domestic work magically reduces once you become a working mother. The family must help more, and you may find you can manage quite well without a daily.

Chores such as cleaning and ironing are done in half the time when you have a job to go to, and better done, as well. I haven't noticed that the homes of working mothers are any dirtier than those of stay-at-home wives. In fact it is the opposite, if anything, as you become tidier and more efficient when you are working.

You may wonder whether your clothes are all right, or whether your hair style is boring and out of date. These are all questions that bother the would-be returner. I wouldn't advise, though, going to the hairdresser for a completely new style, or refurbishing your wardrobe, until you are established in your new job, and have a clearer idea of what will be suitable for your new image. Mostly, you need to feel comfortable, and there is a risk that you may buy an executive suit that is just too smart.

Doctors, lawyers, broadcasters, all tend to dress very casually indeed for work, in track suits or jumpers and skirts, so you don't have to turn up on your first day looking like an air hostess. You will soon notice what the others are wearing, and dress so that you fit in. I wouldn't buy a new outfit to start work in, but save money until I'd got my eye in.

Don't ever worry, either, that your new working life is going to make you tired, or old before your time. The exact reverse will happen, and you will find yourself wonderfully rejuvenated and possessing new-found energy levels. As time goes on, you will find – or others will tell you – that your voice even takes on a perkier and more confident tone. You will very likely lose weight as well, as there's now no time for nibbles, and your general health will improve.

This all comes from an increased sense of purpose and self-worth. Mrs Jehan Sadat, widow of President Anwar Sadat, lives by the motto that busy people are happy people. In her view, you can hardly be too busy, so long as you are convinced of the usefulness of what you are doing. It is boredom, not having enough to do, that brings about depression, dullness and hastens old age and decrepitude. Those who do fulfilling jobs will simply never have time to be bored. This also means less time to complain, gossip and all the other time-wasting activities those without enough to do tend to indulge in.

The new working woman is, without doubt, a great improvement on her stay-at-home predecessor.

Further Reading and Information

Returners, Elizabeth Dobbie (NACCW, Drayton House, 30k Gordon Street, London WC1H 0AX.)

The Unemployment Handbook, Guy Dauncey (National Extension College, Cambridge).

Futurewoman, Shirley Conran and Elizabeth Sidney (Penguin, 1982). Valuable chapter entitled 'Do You Sincerely Want to Work?'

WOW and TOPS Courses, information from your local Job Centre.

Manpower Services Commission, Training Division, Moorfoot, Sheffield, S1: free booklets on re-entry and retainer schemes.

The Third Hand, Joan Eastman, 6 St Vincent's Road, Bristol, BS8 4PS: refresher courses and part-time work for social workers.

Association of Women Solicitors, Eva Crawley, 4 The Hexagon, Fitzroy Park, London N6: refresher courses for solicitors wishing to return to work.

National Advisory Centre for Women, Drayton House, 30k Gordon Street, London WC1H 0AX.

5

Retraining

At some stage, you may well feel you would like a career that is different from the one you originally chose. You may consider retraining for another profession if:

- You decide your present job is no longer satisfying;
- You have 'outgrown' it;
- You have been made redundant, and there are few opportunities for similar work in your area;
- You would like a proper career now that your family's needs require less full-time commitment.

In each case you will have to ask yourself the same set of questions before embarking on a possibly expensive and protracted course of training. These are: what amount of time can I spend training for a new career; how much will it all cost; what likelihood is there of a good job at the end of it all; and, most important, what kind of job would I most like to do?

Whatever your reasons for wanting to retrain, if you are at all unclear about your suitability or aptitude for a particular job or career path, I would strongly recommend investing in a professional careers analysis. You can do this to some extent for yourself by drawing up on a sheet of paper all the things you like doing, and those on which you are less keen. But a professional analysis will often uncover aspects of yourself of which you were only dimly aware.

You may want to undertake a long course of academic training, but a career test could show that you are not suited to this. Conversely, you may be considering taking a low-level job, while a career test can show that you are a frustrated high-flyer. You may like the idea of a rural job, yet all tests could indicate that you are basically a city type. The psychological tests used in careers analyses are very accurate, and have been developed over several years. Those who know exactly what they want to do, of course, and will not entertain anything else, would be wasting their time and money on such a test.

Career analyses take about six hours altogether, and involve a detailed questionnaire you fill in at home, and a series of aptitude tests taken at the Centre. You will get your results the same day, and they can be surprising and vastly encouraging. They do not depend on what you have done before, as they test innate aptitude and tendencies rather than what you may have learned in examinations. For instance, all my life I have just assumed I was practically innumerate, yet a mini-careers test I took showed me to have a reasonable ability at numbers, though no genius it must be said. Many women, particularly, go through their lives assuming they are bad at things, just because they had a poor experience of the subject when at school.

A career analysis will pinpoint your strengths and weaknesses, and also suggest specific career paths, and tell you how to go about training for the job you would like. The consultant will also advise on whether there would be many openings in your proposed profession for somebody of your age, type, and locality. Up to the age of 45 at least, you can think of making a major change in your career. After that, it may be more difficult, simply because employers will be less ready to take you on. There is a big difference between being determined and being pigheaded: a career test may well highlight this in a way you can accept.

Nearly, though not absolutely, always, changing direction will involve a period of training. We are very lucky in Britain in that there is a very wide and ever-expanding range of possibilities for the mature person to retrain. Never feel that an early, wrong decision will blight you for life. Nor need you assume that, because you already have a degree or professional qualification, you must follow this for the rest of your life. One friend of mine qualified as a water pollution expert then, at the age of 30, decided she wanted to be an actress. Another acquaintance trained as a dentist, then developed an interest in antique clothes. She studied dressmaking and the antique clothes market, and eventually opened up her own shop. It was the culmination of a dream and is doing very well indeed.

Yet another woman trained as an air hostess, and later landed a job in local radio. A fourth friend, also a former air hostess, is now a senior executive with a public relations company. There are endless possibilities, but none of them will just happen.

Never, ever, let lack of money put you off training for a worthwhile career. Many retraining programmes are completely free and on several full-time ones, there is a useful grant available. Single parents that I know, with no other source of income, have supported themselves and their children on a mature students grant. It is rare that grants would be available for part-time study, and you can't keep on getting them – usually only one major award in a lifetime is permitted. You are entitled to that one, however, so if you didn't take advantage of it when you left school, you can do so now.

Even a career which involves long and intensive training, such as becoming a doctor, can be undertaken in later life. Dr Chandra Patel, the Croydon GP who has become famous for her work on biofeedback techniques, was 26 and married with a family before she undertook medical training. She did not find it easy to secure a place at a London medical school, but applied and applied and applied. They took her in the end.

If you are somebody who left school early, and without many qualifications, perhaps now is the time to make up that lack. There are certainly no grounds for thinking you can't pass exams, just because you didn't do all that well at school. Studies on the subject indicate that people who couldn't pass GCE at 16 can very often sail through these exams at a later age, when school-type pressures are over. There is also no evidence for the idea that women are any less intelligent than men, though you might think so from taking a look at relative professional qualifications and positions. It is the case though that, very often, girls become discouraged and disillusioned at an early age and it can take them a very long time to unlearn negative attitudes.

Some people may worry that, if they embark on a course of training, they will be the only mother, grandmother, or woman over 25 on the course. It may have been rare to spot mature students 20 years ago, but now they are very numerous, and you will not at all be out of place. More men than ever before are making career changes in mid life, too, and it is an ever-increasing trend to learn new skills at an older age. Some women are even – literally – going back to school and taking O- and A-levels in the classroom along with their sons and daughters. Not all would welcome this idea, of course, but it is a possibility if there are no suitable day or evening classes for adults in your area.

Age need never be a stumbling block to study, and would only be a serious consideration where you would be too old for the eventual career. Anybody over 25 would be daft to consider a career in ballet or other dancing, as the tragic Zelda Fitzgerald, wife of novelist Scott, did. But in many careers, such as social work, medicine or teaching, maturity is actually an asset.

There is also a good chance of a worthwhile job at the end of it since employers can see that, off your own bat, you have pursued a course of study and gained high qualifications.

One very big growth area for women is the health field. Though around 80 per cent of practising doctors in the NHS are male, an increasing number of women are deciding to train in the ever-expanding alternative fields, such as acupuncture, homoeopathy, massage or herbal medicine. Women very often discover in themselves a gift for healing, but this may not emerge until they are in their twenties or thirties. However, there are very many opportunities to train in these fields, and the services of good alternative practitioners are very much in demand. This is one profession where maturity is almost considered a qualification in itself, and is one where women are very much coming to the fore. One reason for this is that the health field benefits very much from having the feminine input.

To practice as a healer in an unorthodox area, you need to be sympathetic, open-minded and non-authoritarian. You do not need long strings of O- and A-levels, or degrees and diplomas, as personality is what counts most.

Not every woman considering retraining will want to work in the health area. I just mention this, as it is not covered in conventional career books at all, but does open up exciting possibilities for women. The Neal's Yard Therapy Rooms in Covent Garden, London, can give you details on training for a wide variety of alternative therapies, and the work itself is varied, satisfying and useful. After all, we can do without many of the artefacts of our modern technological society, but we can't be happy without health. Healing is something which can be taken up at any age, though it is not recommended before about 25.

Be that as it may, before deciding on any retraining programme, whether long or short, you will need to take a long look at your possible future life. If you are thinking about a new career, it will have to be one that will last you a long time, rather than being a short-term solution which will put you back in the same non-career position five years later.

So do look for opportunities that will offer good continuing prospects and a proper career structure. Bear in mind that, if you are thinking about part-time work, it is always more difficult to find responsible and stimulating posts on a less than full-time basis. It is true that Frances Cairncross, formerly Women's Editor of *The Guardian*, was able to do this on a part-time basis, but she had already fully established herself first.

It is also important to consider the likelihood of your getting a good job once you have completed training. Always think ahead to the career, rather than stopping at the study or training. Though study can be rewarding in itself, unless it leads on to something definite the satisfaction will be short-lived. Ideally, study should not be seen as an end in itself for the older person, unless you are over 50 and don't really want another full-time job.

Training for a new career first involves sitting down and examining all the possibilities on offer. As a very first step, you could go to your nearest Job Centre, just to get some idea of the kind of jobs that are being offered in your area. Some local offices also provide Job Libraries, with information on a whole range of occupations. Those who are undecided about what to do for the best may find something here to fire their imaginations.

Most moves to a different career will involve at least some training, so while you are at the Job Centre, ask about TOPS schemes, and get their range of leaflets. Just sitting at home one evening reading through all this literature will almost certainly help to clarify your thoughts.

Those most in need of examining the realistic possibilities are women who have been made redundant. Often then, a new career choice will be forced on you by circumstances. If the clothing factory where you worked has closed down, for example, there would be little likelihood of your existing skills being of much use on the commercial market. Women who have been made redundant and don't intend to sit round at home all day will probably be highly motivated to look for a new job, and to use the opportunity as a period of growth, and to qualify themselves for something better. Also, redundancy often brings severance pay, which could be useful to tide you over while you are making up your mind.

Women who have been away from work for a long time may need to ease themselves in gently, before even going on a course of study. The WOW courses, available in several parts of the country, and mentioned in the previous chapter, could be ideal for you. These courses are also just the thing for those women who, while knowing what they would like to do, are nervous about re-entering the working world, and would like to build confidence first. WOW courses are intended to break you in gently, and introduce you to the working environment as it really is.

Anybody who has had a period away from work due to disablement or illness, can discuss possible new openings with the Disablement Resettlement Officer. Her job is to know about all the training schemes and available jobs for people who are less than 100 per cent able-bodied. You could well find that there are a surprising amount of jobs open to you, and these are more wide-ranging than you might imagine.

It is worth taking full advantage of any facilities that are going, especially the ones that cost nothing. You can only ever gain, never lose. A few enquiries at the right time could even pave the way to an exciting new career for you.

The next thing is to look at the job you have been doing, or last did, and ask yourself whether there is anything you can salvage from it. As it is always easier to build on existing skills than to learn completely new ones, try to remember which aspects you enjoyed most, and the ones you liked least.

Let us suppose that you were an air hostess. As this is a finite kind of job, with a definite lifespan of its own, many ex-hostesses will be looking for other jobs in later life. Did you enjoy the actual travel, the uniform, the feeling of working for a big company, the chance to meet lots of people, however briefly, or the service and caring aspect? Settle on the ingredient which gave you the greatest thrill and consider whether there is any way you can build on this. Some people like the security and sense of belonging that comes from working for a huge company. Some women enjoy wearing a uniform, and having the sense of status that that brings. Others like to be on the move all the time, and would like a travelling type of job. Maybe a sales job would suit you, or a job in a travel agency.

Perhaps you were a nurse. Did you enjoy most helping patients, being an authority figure, the sense of comradeship that went with working in a hospital? Did you like the drama, the doctors, making people better?

If you were a dancer, did you like the dressing-up, the rehearsals, the satisfaction of mastering a new routine, actually being in front of an audience? Any of these attributes, while not formal skills, are realized when on the job, and could influence your future decisions. Try never to throw away all your old skills, even if you hated your previous job. Hotel work is something many young girls choose and then leave not long afterwards. If you were a short-lived hotel receptionist, try to remember what made you choose this job in the first place. Some people love working in warm, comfortable interiors, while others prefer to be outdoors. We are all different, and when choosing a second career, it should be planned more carefully than the first, especially if the first didn't last long.

When thinking back to your last job, also itemize in your mind the reasons why you left it. What *didn't* you like about it? Whatever it was, try not to let the same mistake happen again. It could if you are not careful, and some people keep choosing the wrong jobs, as others marry and remarry Mr Wrong.

A job, after all, is part of you, so let it be an extension of your true personality. Those who are square pegs in square holes are happiest in life. You don't want to go to tremendous effort to find a new job, only to discover not long afterwards that you hate it as much as you did the original one.

It is essential also for you to realize just how important, or unimportant, money and position are to you. The most rewarding jobs aren't by any means always the best paid, or the ones that offer the most spectacular ladder climb. But it may be important for you that the career you have in mind pays well. If so, find out before it's too late what the pay scales are. Social work and teaching do not, on the whole, offer material rewards beyond the dreams of avarice, whereas acting, for the lucky few, can.

As a fully trained doctor you will find the rates of pay high, but the study is long and arduous. Journalists can be paid anything from peanuts to a superstar salary. As a beginner in any job, whatever your age, you will probably be paid at the bottom rate, so don't expect money to flood in all at once.

Right. You have now decided on the job you would like, and the career structure that seems suitable and realistic. The next step is to find out exactly which training facilities are available on your doorstep. You may well discover there are all sorts of courses going on that you didn't even know about, as most people are only dimly aware of the extremely wide range of training courses going on at the local colleges.

The good thing about revitalizing your skills, or learning new ones, is that this can very often be done part-time, in conjunction with an existing job, or while bringing up children. Very many courses on offer for women take childcare problems into account, and there may well be a crèche. As you are unlikely to have much money to spare while retraining it is a good idea to fit this in with an existing job, if at all possible. Not everybody will be able to do this and by no means are all courses part-time. You couldn't, for instance, try to train as a doctor while working at something else, but you could become an accountant simply by persevering with evening classes. For those still in work but anxious to change direction, try at least to start your new training before handing in your notice. If this cannot be done, get the course properly fixed up before leaving your present job.

If you are housebound with small children, you can at least take your preliminary exams, if these are necessary, to get you started on your course of study. Before embarking on a very time-consuming course, it may be an idea to discover whether you actually like studying, if you have not done much of this in the past. A good way of finding this out before you have burned too many boats, would be to attend classes given by Adult Education Colleges, and the Workers' Educational Association. Other institutions offering evening courses are art galleries, photographic clubs and extramural departments of universities. You could sign up for a subject that particularly interests you, just to see whether you can cope with sitting captive for an hour listening to somebody else speak. Not everybody does, by all means.

Courses like this may help you to find out whether something you may have pursued as a hobby, such as photography, could lead at all to a professional career. A preliminary class could also assist you in establishing whether you would enjoy doing this full-time.

Some colleges to further education also run 'back to study' courses, to get you back into the swing of working in this way. The National Extension College in Cambridge has correspondence courses designed to help those considering further study. You may, for example, be considering a science or maths course, in which case you can take a special adult 'taster' course in maths, physics, or general science. Many jobs these days require O- and A-levels, though these do become less important the older you get. But if you do need some specific GCEs as a preliminary to entering a formal study course, you will find almost all subjects are offered by local adult colleges. Some adults, in particular those who left school many, many years ago, may feel that GCEs are too 'childish' for them. In this case, there are several colleges, both residential and non-residential, which offer courses specially designed for grown-ups. A list is given at the end of this chapter.

A large proportion of adult courses are grant-aided. A booklet, *State Bursaries for Adult Education: Courses in long-term residential colleges*, is available from the Department of Education and Science, Awards 11, Honeypot Lane, Stanmore, Middlesex. For purely academic study, you will probably be entitled to a grant only if you are pursuing a full-time course.

In later life, women sometimes come to feel they have missed out by not having a degree. Before signing up for a three-year degree course, ask yourself why you didn't take one in the first place, and why you would like to do so now.

It is a fact that a degree hardly ever leads straight to a job, and this is particularly the case in the type of degrees that are commonly taken by mature women, such as English, philosophy and psychology. I meet many women, either single parents, housewives or those encumbered by children, who embark on degree courses without having the slightest idea of why they are doing them. You hear answers like 'it was a whim,' or, 'I needed to keep my brain active,' and so on. One woman said: 'People keep asking what I'm going to do with my degree, but I'm not interested in what I shall be doing in the future, only what I'm doing now.'

There is nothing theoretically wrong with these reasons, and if you keep seeing your life in terms of the future, you may end up by never living now at all. But, the danger is that, if you are finding only a temporary palliative, and you are killing time rather than using it, your happiness and employability will not be increased in the slightest.

A common contemporary situation, at least among middle-class

h, is this: an unambitious girl leaves school at 16 to work in a bank.
rries almost the first male she meets, at the age of 19 or 20. She
immediately leaves work to start a family. Ten years later she finds
herself bored and frustrated, wondering what on earth she has done with
her life. Determined to do something, she signs up for an A-level or two,
and passes them. This encourages her to do a degree course. She signs up
for a three-year Arts Degree and, in the meantime, gets divorced. After
receiving her BA, she looks round for a job, only to discover she is as
unemployable as before.

With increasing depression, she finds that the only jobs she is offered
are ones that are way below what she now considers her qualifications to
be, and she cannot earn enough to support herself and her children.
What does she do? Common modern heartaches like these could be
avoided if women who find themselves in this position first took a
careers analysis, or a WOW course, or assessed job possibilities in their
area beforehand.

A common job-delaying tactic is the 'have another baby' syndrome,
as described by Colette Dowling in her uncomfortably near-the-
knuckle book, *The Cinderella Complex*. It is very common indeed for
women to take a degree and then on attaining their BA or BSc, to have
another baby straight away. There is not really a lot of sense in taking a
degree unless you intend to do something constructive with it. It should
not be seen merely as a way of getting through the next three years. The
other, very important, point is that taking degrees and having babies
does not lead to eventual independence, which is what qualifications and
courses should ideally equip you for.

If you don't want independence, what do you want? It is as well to try
and come to terms with your reasons for wanting to retrain, and realize
that any study course is essentially preparatory to something else. Unless
it is undertaken with a positive end in view, it tends to be undervalued,
and soon forgotten.

Women who have been housebound and tied to drudgy jobs for a
number of years, or those who have been in routine jobs, can find a
college course a very exciting new departure. As a preliminary to
proper, paid work it can be life-enhancing and get your brain ticking
over once more. But I can't help feeling that college courses should be
taken with a view to getting you back into the outside world where,
henceforth, you will stay. If you scuttle straight back into the home and
wonder whatever to do next, then something has gone wrong.

Degree courses entitle you to a grant, even if you are a married
woman and therefore, notionally at least, being supported by a man. The
Open University is the best known of all degree institutions for adults,

and its standards are quite as high as those demanded by more conventional universities.

There are no formal entry qualifications as such, and new students begin with a foundation course designed to serve as a gentle introduction to the subjects you will be studying in depth. The Diploma of Higher Education (Dip HE) is a two-year course attracting a large number of mature students, where the qualification is intended to be useful in its own right. You should find out from your local library, Citizens' Advice Bureau or Job Centre, which colleges in your area, if any, are offering these very useful courses. Always ask in advance for prospectuses, and request an interview when you are not sure which course would be best for you, or are wondering which would lead to a direct job qualification.

A growing number of adult colleges have now begun to offer Start Afresh courses, especially for women who want to return to work, or take a new direction in their lives. One such pioneer course run at Manchester Polytechnic, and funded by the Equal Opportunities Commission, gives information on educational, training and employment opportunities, and outside visits are arranged for women interested in such jobs as social services or computer programming. A crèche is provided at this course.

Clare Debenham, the Community Liaison Officer at Manchester Poly, said: 'A lot of women feel they have nothing much to offer. Some have qualifications and some don't. The course caters for all women and is aimed at developing self-confidence in taking the difficult step of starting afresh.' Your local college may well have a course very similar to this one: it's worth making enquiries. If they haven't embarked on such a course, perhaps you could suggest one. If enough students request a course, any course, adult colleges will look seriously at the question of offering one.

You may have passed all these preliminary stages already, and have the educational entry qualifications ready for your new career. You may now be in a position to start training for a specific job, and this can be done in a variety of ways. You may take a full-time vocational course, a part-time day release or evening course, a correspondence course, or do on-the-job training. You would have to decide, from the options available, which type of course would best suit your purposes, and your pocket.

Very many firms, particularly those in computing and the more technological spheres, offer on-the-job training. Several girls with very few O-levels have found that they can pick up computer programming quite easily, with a small amount of basic instruction. One girl, now working with a large computer company, said: 'I only had three O-levels, and imagined computers were another world, quite beyond me. But I found it was easy enough to pick up, and I often stay on my computer after work hours, as I enjoy it so much.' Her firm provided training while she was employed, with full pay.

There is now a definite move to attract women into management positions, and with less than ten per cent of managers being women, this is not before time. Some large firms will send their bright, ambitious girls into special all-women management courses, and pay for their training.

I once attended such a course run by Eleanor Macdonald, an enterprising septuagenarian, who has now run very many such training programmes. It was quite an eye-opener. We had a mock boardroom meeting, where strategies that men employ were revealed. Confidence and effectiveness skills were also imparted. Since Eleanor Macdonald pioneered these courses, many women-into-management courses have been instigated, and they are generally very successful. Your job is to persuade your firm you are worth sending on one of these courses.

The famous TOPS courses are designed for those who know already exactly what they want to do jobwise. They are run by the Training Services Division of the Manpower Services Commission, and offer more than 500 courses in different parts of the country. There are various levels of course, ranging from simple clerical skills to professional, high-powered management training. You can also take preparatory courses in Maths and English, if you feel these might let you down. Should you be interested in learning a manual trade or craft, these can be arranged in Skillcentres, or actually at employers' premises. An increasing number of women are now turning to previously all-male occupations, such as electrician, plumber, car mechanic, builder, and doing very nicely as well. A girl with a bent for such work can find opportunities to train quite easily, and she need never worry about being out of work later.

Such practical skills are in very great demand, as there are few people about who are genuinely good plumbers, builders and decorators. It's said that in a very male-dominated job you have to be ten times as good as a man to succeed. As someone before me said, luckily that't not very difficult. You would not have to be a genius to be better than the average plumber or workman!

To be eligible for a TOPS course, you must be over 19 and have left school or full-time education for more than two years. Those who want help with a postgraduate course have to be over 27, and there is theoretically no upper age limit, though you may not be allowed on some courses if your chances of finding a job are remote owing to your age. For computer training, for example, you should be under 35, and the over forties can be offered courses in catering, accounts and salesmanship, where age is so much less of a barrier.

You would have to undergo an aptitude test, and must also fully intend to take a job at the end of your training period. So no have-another-baby thoughts should be entertained here. TOPS courses are full-time and very serious affairs, lasting from three weeks to a year. After taking one, you would not be eligible for another for three years at least.

There are many different TOPS courses, and leaflets available for different parts of the country, as the same jobs would not be on offer nationwide. There are also TOPS support schemes for other vocational courses, but they must all be able to lead directly to a job, without further training being necessary. If you are interested in a TOPS course – and don't despise them at all, as they can be wonderful back-to-work motivators – ask in the first instance for an appointment with the Employment Advisor responsible for the courses, at your nearest Job Centre. Some courses are extremely popular, and you may not be able to get on the one you want straight away.

Another type of vocational training may be offered at colleges of further education. You should look here for courses leading to a qualification such as City and Guilds or Royal Society of Arts. Typing, upholstery, interior decorating, are all among the kinds of courses available under this scheme. This is a good one to consider if you have acquired competence in a particular craft during the at-home years, and would now like to turn it into a professional qualification.

There is now a great deal of interest in less mass-produced, more crafty items, but as yet they are not really big money spinners, and tend to be labour-intensive. However, there could be interesting work obtainable in these areas. Upholsterers, tailors and dressmakers may be retained by large firms to carry out this kind of work. There is also the distinct possibility of setting up your own business once you have mastered a craft, an avenue that will be explored further in Chapter Six.

There are many other vocational courses, such as those run by the Technical Educational Council, the Institute of Medical Laboratory Sciences, and the Institute of Electrical and Electronic Engineering Technicians. Diplomas awarded by these institutes are at A-level standard, and are very much geared towards job training. In some cases, they can offer direct jobs with the industry concerned.

Two traditionally popular jobs for older women, or those wanting to improve their professional status, are social work and teaching. Social workers are always needed, and you can easily train over the age of 25. After this age, GCEs would not normally be needed, but you must indicate your ability to pursue a serious course of study. Those between the ages of 21 and 25 would need five O- and two A-levels, to be considered for training. Courses for mature students last for two years, but some colleges have three year courses with a shorter day, for those with family commitments. The qualification obtained at the end of the course is the Certificate of Qualification in Social Work, and this directly qualifies you to work for a Social Service department in residential work, the probation service, educational or charity work. You should not find it too difficult to get a job after completing training.

Though social work is in many ways suitable for older women, only consider it if you feel this is something you would really enjoy. The work can be frustrating, nerve-racking and requiring a high degree of commitment. Also, it is not famous for being extremely well paid, so you must take into account the importance of a good salary afterwards. Most of the women I know who qualified as social workers in later life, found it was quite simple to fit the study in with a young family, and discovered it wasn't too difficult either to obtain interesting jobs after qualifying.

Teaching used to be the cliché job for women who wanted to return to work after spending several years at home. Fifteen years ago, mature students were being very much encouraged to come back to teaching, or to consider this as a late-start career. The situation is very different now, as many areas are not recruiting, and very many teacher training colleges have closed down over the past ten years. On the face of it, teaching may seem like an ideal 'woman's job', as it offers short hours, long holidays, and work in a relatively known environment, with children, who are supposed to be a woman's preserve, after all.

But teaching should never be considered a last-resort job, for those who can't think of anything else to do. There are too many teachers like this already, without adding to their numbers. If you feel you will enjoy teaching, and would like to be successful in it, then it could be the career for you. But it should be chosen for positive, not negative, reasons. Teaching can be a wonderful job for those with the right personality, but hell for those whose heart is not in it. Having a family is not qualification enough for considering this career: very many parents don't actually like children very much at all.

Relevant questions to ask yourself before signing up for a teaching course are: do I sincerely like children enough to want to spend all day with them? Do I enjoy any academic subject enough to want to teach it? This is very important indeed, as a teacher with a genuine love of her subject can be so inspiring to her pupils. I was lucky enough to have, for seven years of my secondary school career, the same English teacher, who imparted such a love of literature that I can still remember her lessons. Other lessons from teachers of other subjects have long been forgotten. I am now passing that love of literature, which has remained, onto my own family.

Teaching is not, I suggest, the job for those who want a glamorous career with individual recognition, who prefer to work with adults, or meet lots of new people all the time. It is not, either, for those who like to be out and about a lot, or who have a low boredom threshold. Many creative people – artists, writers, potters – find that a certain amount of teaching gives them the time to continue their own craft, and provides a welcome balance between working at home and getting out of the house.

Teaching jobs are scarcer than they were, so you would need to find out whether you would be offered a job at the end of the course. Against that it must be said that there are always bound to be a lot of people around who need teaching, so the need for well-qualified teachers can never entirely vanish. There are also very many possibilities within teaching – it doesn't necessarily have to be in a school. It is a very flexible type of career but please don't choose it unless you long to be a teacher above everything else.

Here are some success stories of women who have decided to retrain for different professions later in life. Margaret was working in an advertising agency when her husband was suddenly offered a job in Australia. At the time, both she and her husband were aged around 30 and had no children. Out in Australia, Margaret found it impossible to get a job and, after a period of wondering just what to do, made up her mind to take an acting course. She attended a college in Sydney and, on returning to England, completed her training on a one-year intensive course specially designed for older students. There, she met many others of her own age group, who had felt they wanted to join the acting profession after trying something else first.

On completing her training, Margaret looked round for some jobs, and was surprised to be offered one straightaway. She did not qualify for a grant while training, as she had already had a major award when at University, but she saved up for her course.

Most of the other students had done the same, though some who had not obtained a grant at the age of 18, got assistance from their local authority. Since training, Margaret has had a variety of jobs though, so far, none has actually earned her a living. She does other work in the meantime, such as typing and book-keeping.

Susan had trained as an actress, but married at the age of 19, and soon had three children, so her career had never got off the ground. Nine years later her husband left her and she needed a profession of her own. She spoke fluent French, and had taught in local schools, but realized she would never progress without proper qualifications. She was accepted as a mature student at a London college, and got a job in a junior school immediately after qualifying. She decided to qualify further, and took an evening course to become a teacher of English as a second language. Susan is now a county advisor for English as a second language, and has held many interesting teaching jobs, working with adults, and also with children who have learning difficulties.

Elaine was formerly a technician in a medical laboratory but, at the age of 29, decided to attend art college as a mature student, where she graduated with first class honours. She specialized in silkscreen printing, and now has her own business selling prints to many big London galleries and shops. She also teaches one day a week.

Joan went to art college in Scotland at the age of 18, and became a painter. After a time she began to feel that her type of art was somewhat out of touch with reality and, later in life, decided to train as a potter. She enrolled at a local college, and was actually selling her wares long before she graduated. After being a struggling artist for many years, she said it was a welcome change actually to be able to sell something. Soon after finishing her course she was also appointed pottery tutor at her college. She now teaches pottery in her home and holds regular exhibitions.

Once you have decided on your career, taken your qualifications, amassed all the training you need, the next step is actually to land that job. Is there anything further you need to know? If you have been on a TOPS course or similar, you will have been pointed firmly in the direction of a job, so your worries should be relatively few. But whatever courses you have been on, and however well prepared you might be, you still have to get the job by your own efforts. If you have never really left work, and have kept your hand in, however desultory that work has been, you will find job hunting less difficult. But those who have had a very long gap away from paid employment might imagine that, after completing training, job offers will suddenly flood onto the doormat. They won't.

You have to regard job seeking as a full-time task in itself, and not be tempted to 'relax' and sink into a stupor. Job hunting will now have to take precedence over all other activities, otherwise you will never get the job you want. You can be 'lucky' and get the first job you apply for, but on average, you get an interview for every 10 jobs you go after, and a job for every 10 interviews you attend.

When you get up in the morning, dress as if going to work. This will, in itself, make you feel more efficient than if you are simply slopping around in jeans all day long. Very often, there is a definite feeling of anticlimax when courses finish. There has been, perhaps for several years, guidance and a structure to your day. Now, suddenly, you find you are on your own once more.

You should draw up a CV, along the lines suggested in Chapter Two, and also draw up a list of people who could act as referees. These should be people with definite standing within the community, such as a vicar, Justice of the Peace or bank manager. Keep your letter of application as brief as possible, on a single sheet of paper, and type rather than write it out. When applying for jobs, don't wait for a reply before sending off the next application. Not all firms reply anyway, and waiting could lead to delays and disappointments. Nor should you wait for 'your' job to be advertised: you could wait for ever.

Instead, write to organizations employing people with your kind of qualifications, and offer yourself. Keep a note of all the jobs you have written off for, and keep copies of all the letters you send off. You may only hear from a very small proportion of the firms you write to, and this can come as a nasty surprise. But don't take it as a sign that nobody wants you. It is indisputable that, the more jobs you apply for, the greater your chances of landing one before very long. Never build up hopes of landing a particular job, but try to remain detached from the whole business. If you hope wildly that this application will surely be successful, you can become very difficult to live with, as well as becoming prone to bad fits of depression.

Anxiety clouds your competence and confidence, so try not to go to interviews in a state of hopeful expectation, but be normal and natural. Nothing puts a prospective employer off more than an obviously desperate applicant coming for a job interview, and attempting to be bright and cheerful. It creates a very dreary impression, somehow.

Money will also be a factor for some people, especially if you are living on redundancy money, maintenance payments, or social security. You have to be as cost effective as possible. Work out how many interviews you can afford to attend, and do ask whether travelling expenses will be paid. *There is nothing wrong with doing this, and it will make you seem efficient, not poor.*

Before going for interview, prepare a list of written questions and answers, as you may be taken off guard. Try to put yourself in the position of the employer. He doesn't want to hear the story of your whole life, so stick to the facts relevant to the job in hand. Dress smartly but for adults, the rule is to dress down, rather than up. Don't have your hair done specially, as it creates an over-eager impression. Aim to arrive half an hour before the interview time, as this gives you leeway if trains, buses or traffic jams hold you up. You can use the spare time to look at notice boards and the reception area, to pick up tips about the kind of company you might be working for. Don't ever aim to arrive exactly on time, as this inevitably makes you anxious before you get there.

When you go for lots of interviews, but never actually land the job, you can come to feel you will never be employed, but this isn't the case. Don't give up, and keep applying and going for interviews.

The important thing to bear in mind is that if you truly want a job, you are bound to get one. But you must have sufficient motivation to work, as jobs these days are not at all easy to get, and may become even more difficult as you get older. There is such a thing as being too pushy, and this should be avoided at all costs, as it is almost as offputting as being painfully shy and insecure. Don't be tempted to ring up the interviewer the same day, or write a letter immediately saying how you would love the job. Let him/her decide, but you can gently remind them of your existence if you have not heard within, say, three months.

You should also decide, at the outset, how far you would like to go in your newly-chosen career. For many women, ambition is fired at last, and they can come to feel that the sky is now the limit.

When Eddie Brennan was first looking for paid work, she was simply seeking a job that would help to pay her son's school fees. But, after a time in the job world, she realized she was at least as good as many people who had never stopped working to bring up a family. She rose to becoming a director of the company she now works for, though eight years ago she would not have called herself an ambitious person.

It is as well to have some plan in mind, though always take into account the fact that circumstances may alter. Always have aims, but be flexible within them. If you become too rigid, you can be unhappy when plans don't materialize. Not every plan will come to fruition – nobody is 100 per cent successful in every single thing they do. Here are some pointers: if you want to train as a junior school teacher do you see yourself a head or deputy head eventually? If a social worker, what sort of job do you envisage as the ceiling? You should always bear in mind the possibilities of each career. Once you set your sights, there may be no stopping you.

In the next chapter, we take a close look at how women arrive at the top, and whether the topmost peak is a comfortable or uncomfortable place to be. Retraining may have uncovered latent ambition – but are you prepared for the long and lonely trek to the top – and what will you find when you get there?

Further Information

The National Extension College: information on improving your qualifications. 18 Brooklands Avenue, Cambridge.

The Open University. Walton Hall, Milton Keynes, MU7 6AA. Information on all kinds of courses, both degree and refresher, with fees and grants available. (Several banks offer loan schemes to help pay for fees, so if a grant is out of the question, enquire at your local branch.)

Advisory Council for Adult and Continuing Education: gives a list and advice on educational guidance and career counselling services. 19a de Montford Street, Leicester LE1.

Adults' courses offering alternatives to O- and A-levels: Hillcroft College, South Bank, Surbiton, Surrey. This is a women's college giving a social studies course which includes computer studies. Mainly residential.

Other colleges taking mature students are:

Coleg Harlech, Gwynedd LL46 2PU.

Co-operative College, Stamford Hall, Loughborough, Leics.

Fircroft College, Bristol Road, Selly Oak, Birmingham 29.

Ruskin College, Oxford.

Plater College, Oxford.

City Lit Centre for Adult Studies, Stukely Street, London WC2, offers a one-year full-time New Horizon Course, plus a part-time course for women with family commitments.

Bradford College, Great Harten Road, Bradford BD7 1AY, has a mature student certificate.

The West London Institute of Higher Education, 300 St Margaret's Road, Twickenham, Middlesex, has a part-time course for adults over 25.

Southwark College, 209 Blackfriars Road, London SE1 8NL has a Careers Foundation in Science Course which leads to a degree course at the City of London Polytechnic.

Lucy Cavendish College, Lady Margaret Road, Cambridge, admits only mature women students, over 25, for first degrees or postgraduate work.

Dorset Institute of Higher Education, Wallisdown Road, Poole, Dorset, has a part-time degree course, requiring two or three half-days a week attendance.

6
Women at the Top

Whenever a woman climbs to the professional top she makes national news, which just shows how rare it still is to be female and in that elevated position.

There are, as we have already seen, a myriad reasons why women tend not to succeed. Huge hurdles are constantly strewn in their way, all along the line. The hurdles are nowadays not so much physical or legal or moral, but attitudinal. Lack of confidence may set in very early in life, when an absence of decisive goals can mean that a girl drifts from job to job, not really knowing where she is at, or what she is doing. But even if a girl keeps her determination going long enough to achieve high scholastic honours and lands herself a good job she will, if she is not very careful indeed, still flounder on the lowly rungs of the ladder.

Women, on the whole, go into male-dominated professions completely unprepared for what they will find. Somehow, the way many organizations and jobs are structured do not seem very suitable for the female psyche. Women can find it hard to understand the game that is being played, and may well have problems in coming to terms with power battles. They soon start to wonder how on earth they will cope.

Women on their way up discover that they must soon start to act in ways for which they have not been trained, if they are to be taken seriously. Little girls are still, on the whole, brought up to be sweet and kind and forgiving, but these qualities, while they may smooth the path of domestic life, are of little value in the highly competitive commercial world. A woman who takes her feminine, appealing qualities into the boardroom may not be taken seriously at all. She could well be asked to make the tea, or take the minutes, even if she is in an executive position.

This very thing happened to the one female executive of a large circulation newspaper. Every now and again, the senior executives would withdraw to a country hotel for a 'think tank' weekend. The lady executive, as the only woman normally present on such occasions, was asked to dress attractively, and take notes of what was being said. Actual secretaries were not allowed, as the meetings were intended to be top secret.

And there again, you can see the male mentality in action: the need for secrecy. Shades of the Black Hand Gang! Few women can see the point of keeping secrets, and this is just one more reason why so few get to the top. To most women, top-level meetings are simply games grown-up men play, as they might table tennis or golf. It all indicates that they are still boys at heart, and women can have difficulty in taking any secret meeting seriously. This is a reason why they are not allowed to be freemasons. Most men understand that the world of commerce and take-over bids is a game as well, but the difference is that they play it for real.

Because women have tended to take a secondary, supportive role in so many aspects of modern life, they still tend to be accorded this position even when, theoretically, they may be on an equal footing. Men have grown up seeing females everywhere in subordinate positions, as mothers in the home deferring to Dad, as secretaries, junior teachers, assistants, receptionists – never the doctor, the head teacher or the boss, or at least, very rarely. So, as they assume their place in the adult world, males can find it extremely difficult to regard women in the workplace as real people.

It is true that things are changing here, as more women enter the professions, but attitudes die very hard.

To the average man, a woman in an executive position remains rather an unknown quantity. Is she going to play the game by the rules, does she in fact know what the rules are, or is she going to break every one? So he watches her very carefully, and notes slip-ups. He wonders whether she is going to show signs of emotional behaviour, or burst into tears. I don't know whether men really do cry less than women, or whether female tearducts are more easily activated than male ones, but it is a fact that nearly every woman in an executive position has felt tears welling up, on occasion.

Some men are so terrified even at the prospect of a woman colleague crying, that they won't promote her in case this happens. For a man, promoting a woman to a senior or executive position is a bit like taking on a foreigner. They may be all right, but how can you be sure? Will women gain the company more orders, or ensure that the sales graph plummets?

You may imagine that, by the eighties, most of these problems would have been sorted out, but they are still rampant. There are very few women at the top of the multinationals and other large organizations simply because this milieu is so very masculine. It is the present-day equivalent of planning and fighting a major military campaign. Boardroom decisions and million-pound takeovers demand exactly the same qualities, strategies and treaties as going to war. There are also the territorial aspirations; again, these come more naturally to men than to women. Would a woman ever understand the essentially war-like nature of big business?

Perhaps not, so, to be on the safe side, better to keep her out.

It would be nice to say that there are now appreciably more women at the top than 20 years ago but, sadly, this is not the case. And we won't *get* more women at the top until there *are* more women at the top. Yes, read that again. It's what I meant to say.

Women won't see themselves in senior positions until they see other women in senior positions. It's a bit like a man having a baby. As he knows no other men have had babies, he concludes that this is impossible. If a woman sees no other females in important positions, she may conclude that it is not possible, under any circumstances, to get there herself.

But women at the top is not like men having babies. One *is* impossible (at least with current technology), the other is not. All women have to do is realize they *can* get there, and beat men at their own game. Then they can start to climb up.

Babies are traditionally blamed for halting female progress up the career ladder, but that must be only part of the answer. A quick look at those women who have made it will show that as many have families as have not. In fact, a woman with husband and children who keeps working is more likely to be given promotion than a lonely spinster. The presence of a family indicates that here is a 'normal' woman, who has done things other women do.

No, I think the answer is more likely to be the other way round. Women don't so much stop climbing because they have babies, as have babies to give themselves a valid reason to get out, and halt their career progress in an acceptable way. It's a point brought out in a book alluded to earlier, *The Cinderella Complex*. Colette Dowling states that highly talented women very often become pregnant in order to avoid anxiety over their careers. They advance to a certain extent, and then find the thicket they have entered has turned into an impenetrable jungle. A way out is made available to them, in the shape of a baby, and they may gratefully take it.

It is very common indeed for women to have a third or even fourth child just when the older ones are safely at school, and she would have been free to take on more career responsibilities.

No woman on a high, or even middling, salary need give up her job to become a full-time parent at home, on financial grounds. But many still do. The reason is, not so much that they are racked with guilt at being away from their children, as that they haven't been able to take the pressures at work. So they gracefully withdraw, and nobody will ever blame them for leaving. Rather, they will be admired, as they are seen as selflessly giving up a good career to be a proper mum at home.

So what are these dreadful pressures that drive so many women away from the workforce, before they have gained a proper foothold? Those involved in a structured profession are greatest. These include big business, the law, architecture, the Civil Service, medicine, and all commercial organizations employing 50 or more people.

When you are young, and have just left university or college, you will very likely find it just as easy as a callow youth of the opposite sex to get a job. Ten years later, however, assuming you are still hanging on somehow, you will find that a large proportion of those bright young female graduates who seemed to have such a good future in front of them, have mysteriously disappeared, and you are in a definite minority. In the meantime, those pimply youths will have gained in confidence to become self-assured middle-management executives, wearing tailored suits and beginning to throw their weight around. This happens mainly because the older men in the organization, those who have already got to the top themselves, are naturally going to take more notice of their own kind than a different species. The senior men look out for the likely lads who are one day very possibly going to head operations, and nurture them along. The office 'uncle' is a very real entity in most corporations.

It is very, very difficult indeed for a gifted young woman to have an office 'uncle'. For one thing, if the woman in question is at all physically attractive – and you don't by any means have to be a raving beauty to be accused of casting couch techniques – the motives of the older man, and even your own, will be severely questioned. It is a golden rule of office life that you do not have an affair with a man who is keeping an avuncular eye on you, but it is almost impossible not to be accused of this, even if no such thought could be further from your mind.

It is very, very common indeed for a middle-aged, high-ranking executive to fancy a female aspirant. It is extremely rare the other way round, so much so that one almost never hears of an older woman in an office fancying a young man. It is very unlikely that a senior woman would ever think of a young man in a sexual context, especially if he were working in the same office, but almost every attractive female I know has, at some stage, been propositioned by a man who is senior to her in the organization. If she turns him down, she may not be promoted; if she accepts him, she is playing a dangerous game indeed.

Either way, the woman is liable to lose. It is very unfortunate that, in our society, there is always likely to be a sexual frisson between young female and older male. Some people feel that this is what keeps life exciting, but I'm sure it is yet another reason why so few women become successful in public life. The story is so common, so universal, so archetypal, so old and so new. Charlotte Brontë ruined her chances in Belgium by falling hopelessly in love with her teacher, Professor Héger, and Madame Héger, his wife, found out. Those older men, when they seem wise and caring, do exert a powerful attraction – still. And for us, brought up in a world where sexual overtones are encouraged all the time, it can be all but impossible to resist. Few women are immune to an invitation to lunch in a secluded place, with a highly attractive older man who just happens to be the boss of the firm.

It is the stuff that romantic fiction is founded on: the most potent stories always tell of a helpless young female who comes up against an irresistible older, worldly, handsome man. So we are bound to apply this fantasy, at least to some extent, in working life. And most people, of whatever sex and age, long to be loved and wanted.

If you react in a human way to problems at work, you may be marked down as emotional. On the other hand, if you remain completely impassive, you risk being called a cold fish. So how should you behave? The problem is, it's not only the men, but other women in an organization can tend to give you the cold shoulder as well. Unfortunately, there has been little solidarity among women in the workforce. This could be changing now, though, as more all-female networks spring up, and we realize the importance of banding together. The only real way to behave in an office is to be yourself: it's impossible to keep any other kind of behaviour up for very long. On the other hand, if you try always to remain positive and cheerful, you will actually become more like this, in time. Don't blame and don't criticize: these are, again, golden rules of successful office behaviour.

From an early age, men learn how to take orders and also how to give them. It's something they pick up in the playground, and continue with team games. It has been noticed by many researchers that women on the whole are not good at, and do not enjoy, team games. They tend not to see themselves as part of a team, working for the common good. Men also learn how to delegate and knuckle under, not to take work problems personally and, as in the army, to obey the uniform and the position, rather than the individual. A man may have personal likes and dislikes at work, but he is careful not to let them show if he is keen to rise within the company.

Women remain more maverick, though they can learn the secrets of male behaviour if they have a mind to. Mrs Thatcher learned it quickly, and look where it got her. Some people have been disappointed that she has done so little to promote the women's cause, and complain that her cabinet consists of hard men. But she would never, ever have become Prime Minister if she had been a feminist – she wouldn't have attracted all those male votes.

We often hear, in newspaper or television reports, that a business-woman has remained very 'feminine'. By this, reporters usually mean that the female executive in question has a nice hairdo, wears lipstick and scent, and speaks in a soft voice. Some women managers even go to the extent of wearing low-cut dresses to emphasize their 'feminine' image. But however fragile they look, if they are heading a big commercial organization you can bet that somewhere along the line, they will have picked up the male techniques, and used them to their own advantage.

They will have learned the rules which say, you take orders from your superior whether or not you agree with him, and you give praise generously, but reserve criticism for yourself. You will also consciously try to keep the morale of your troops high. You will have learned to keep company policy close to your chest, to know how to hire and fire, to be able to tell a lesser employee when his or her work is not up to scratch. You will have learned how to delegate, how to present a united front with your fellow executives, how to separate yourself from your work.

You will have learned not to take criticism personally, not to wear your heart on your sleeve, and to cultivate friendships and acquaintances that further your career, rather than liking colleagues just for their own sakes. Unless you are prepared to abide by these rules, you won't ever get to the top of a mighty corporation, however clever you are at your actual work. It needs very special talents to become a top-flight executive, and these come harder for most women.

Being a senior executive does *not* mean you have to become a horrible person, and create an atmosphere of fear and terror all around you. Women who do this are very unsure of themselves, and try to instil fear into subordinates as a form of self-defence. Not only is it not necessary, it should never, ever be considered behaviour to aim at.

One of the most effective female executives I have ever come across is Felicity Green. Physically very small and frail-looking, Felicity worked her way to senior executive positions from being a humble secretary. She has been on the board of Mirror Group Newspapers, a senior director of the Vidal Sassoon Company, and associate editor of the Daily Express. Her main quality is that she is always positive. She also always remains pleasant, and makes you feel you are the best worker she has ever had. She exemplifies the law that you do not have to be nasty to succeed in business – just positive and determined.

In any walk of life, to be successful, you have to believe in yourself, and even if you are feeling depressed, take care not to communicate this to others. It only makes them lose the confidence they formerly placed in you.

Some women simply thrive on success, and look younger and healthier all the time. Felicity Green, consultant surgeon Margaret Ghilchik, and Pineapple Dance Studios boss Debbie Moore are all very different women indeed, but they all have this in common, that they exude the feeling they love what they are doing, are in complete control, and would not rather be doing anything else. Successful people always look happy, and in fact you cannot expect to succeed if you go round with a face like a wet weekend.

Before you can get to the top, or even ascend many rungs of the ladder, you need to have a very clear idea of what life will be like there, and whether this is what you would like. Some people don't, and there is nothing wrong with that. Like any mountain, the air is always rarefied at the top, and the summit is a lonely place to be. Gossip and chumminess will have to take second place, and your career must always come first.

You will never get into a managerial position by accident. You must want it above all else, plan for it, and be prepared to forego other short term achievements to arrive at your chosen place. You should always keep your eventual destination in mind as you travel. But don't ever expect 'the top' to be a comfortable place. As things are these days, you will almost certainly find that there are others who attempt to undermine you, and some who resent your success. You have to see this all as very much part of the game, and detach yourself from it, otherwise you could become overwhelmed by the pressures. This necessary detachment is still a problem for many women who can tend to identify themselves far too closely with the job, so that they become personally affronted when things go wrong. But this is the business world we're talking about – women who easily retire hurt may not be of the right type to climb in an organization.

I have met some rather sad female executives who are really unsure of themselves and their position. The very worst executives of all – and there are plenty of men like this as well – are those who take all credit for themselves, and immediately pass on blame to their staff. As you are responsible for your staff, you should never blame them, but always be big enough to say: it was my fault for not ordering enough stock (or whatever).

Perhaps you have assiduously climbed to the top, taken note of all the rules of the game, and are now finding your position very barren and uncomfortable. Perhaps you don't like it all that much now you are there.

Many an executive, male as well as female, has painfully ascended to the topmost rung and then said to themselves: is this all? Is this really it? It is unlikely that you could get all the way to the top without realizing what you are letting yourself in for, but assuming you are now having second thoughts, what should you do?

I think that here you have to ask yourself some searching questions, such as: why have I been so anxious to get to the top? Why is it not what I expected? Why am I not happy here? Just asking those questions will tend to give you the answers. It may be the absence of female company that makes you feel lonely and abandoned, or the ruthlessness, or the cut-throat competition. Then you must ask yourself whether there is anything you can change for the better.

When the answer to this is no – and many organizations have very rigid structures – and there is no possibility of changing the structure round to suit yourself, then you will probably have to leave, either to join another organization, or to start up your own business. Women can be extremely successful at this, and it is an alternative we will discuss in detail later in the chapter.

Anybody who feels she is not being valued in her present job should be prepared to move somewhere else. Similarly, any woman who is not really happy where she is should consider a move. Life is too short to be spent in a job, or with a company, you no longer like. Nearly everybody who becomes extremely successful is prepared to move around a bit. So do change companies, change jobs, change direction, as all change must mean growth, and adds impetus to your life. As any good career is bound to encompass a large part of your life, it's never enough to dismiss it with 'it's only a job'. All high fliers, potential and actual, give far more to their job than merely a nine to five commitment. They give more than they absolutely have to, both in terms of time and effort. It is a factor with all those who achieve career success. And it's one reason why women, when they plead for more part-time possibilites, will never achieve ultimate success. A career has to come first, if it is to hit the heights.

It has always been accepted that a man will give a large part of his life, thought, and time to his career. For a man, his career or profession almost *is* him, in a way it has never been for a woman. In the game *Happy Families*, we meet Mr Bun the Baker, but Mrs Bun is always the baker's wife. Whenever you meet a man, the first question asked is what he does. A job has always very closely defined a man, and nobody minds if their profession unashamedly comes first in their life.

For a woman, however, it is quite a new concept that her job should be vitally important to her. There is often a subtle distinction made between women who 'have' to work, and those who work because they 'want' to. The former are seen as brave souls, battling against the odds in a hostile world, but the latter can easily be seen as self-indulgent, putting themselves first, before the needs of family and husband.

This attitude is lessening all the time, but vestiges of it remain, and you may still have to combat it. It is still the case that a man can go to work at the other end of the world, and his wife will, in many cases, automatically follow him. But how often does it happen the other way round? Many, many women are living in places where they have not chosen to be, simply because of their husband's job. Yet very few men indeed exist in places they have not chosen, because their wife's job has taken them there.

Similarly, nobody ever asks how a man manages to fit his job in with a family, but it is often the first question that is asked of a career woman.

Women are not supposed to mind if their husbands earn more than they do, but men are assumed to be justified in feeling resentful if their wives are the major earners. Similarly, nobody raises an eyebrow if a woman gives up her career to accompany her husband to another location.

So, whereas a man will not normally have to ask himself whether his career will fit in with his wife and family, a woman will almost always have to come to terms with this. If there is a conflict of interests, whose should take precedence? Should the job come first, or the family? Should the wife's, or the husband's career, be considered the more important one? A woman who aims to make a success of her career will not have to do heartsearching to find the answers. If there is a conflict, her job is as important as his. The job comes first, and the family will fit in, should be her answer.

Once you have told yourself that your career, to you at least, comes first, then it's surprising how easily other aspects of your life fall into place. In my experience, there is no problem at all juggling home, family, children, and a career. School prize and sports days come round only once a year, and you can always take these out of holiday entitlement, if you feel you must attend. Similarly, children of dedicated working mothers are hardly ever ill. It's the kids of stay-at-home mothers who are always in bed with 'flu, or chicken pox, or something. Working mothers don't expect their children to be ill, and they respond by keeping well.

What if your husband doesn't like you working late, bringing work home, or expects to have his meal on the table when he gets in from work? Well, all I can say is that, if you have encouraged a man in this sort of behaviour, you have only yourself to blame. You teach people how to treat you – everybody does – and if you are treated like a doormat, this means you must behave like one.

There should be no real conflict of interests, and I don't think that in an absolute sense, either the job or the family will have to come first. It is a matter of taking each situation on its individual merits. If you sometimes have to work doubly hard, there will be other times when you can slacken off a bit, so it is all a matter of monitoring very carefully your commitment to each aspect of your life. Running a family in tandem with a job need not drive you apart, mentally. The problems involved have been very over-emphasized, and few people have concentrated on the advantages, which are many. These days, children tend to be far more proud of having a mother who has kept her own career, than if she stays at home all the time. It seems to impart some extra status to children, and also makes them more independent from an early age. If they can't be fetched and carried all over the place, it's marvellous how they manage to find alternative transport.

Running your own business

It is not easy – and nobody should pretend it is – for women to arrive at the top in traditional professions, or in large hierarchical companies. The rules there have been established by men, for men, and women have to fit in. But running your own business is different. This is an area wide open for women, and if you run your own show, you can do it your way. If you prefer co-operation to competition, this is how you can organize things. If you want to work part-time, you can, or if you want to work seven days a week, 12 hours a day, this is entirely your decision.

There is a saying: nobody got rich working for somebody else, and there is truth in this. Many, many women have proved that they can run their own businesses very successfully indeed. I could, if given a minute or two, rattle off the names of most of the women at the top of professions like law and medicine, or who are senior company directors. But I couldn't even begin to list those who have established their own thriving businesses, as there are so many of them.

Why is it that so many women can succeed in running their own outfit, whereas such a high proportion get nowhere in the employed world? It's because women do not, on the whole, readily adjust to the patriarchal, rigid structures of big business corporations, but when it comes to starting and running their own enterprise and they can please themselves, they flourish.

It's said that around 80 per cent of new businesses go bust very quickly after starting up, but those being run by women have a far lower bankruptcy rate. One of the reasons for this is that, when a man imagines running his own business, he often sees himself driving a car, smoking a fat cigar, having property all over the place, a desk bristling with telephones and machines, and a glamorous secretary.

He will often acquire these artefacts long before his business is properly established. A woman, by contrast, hardly ever goes on one of these anticipatory ego-trips. Instead of having to have a prestige office suite with a big desk, she will be quite happy to work in a garden shed, or corner of her bedroom. Usually, she is not particularly interested in having a company car or glossy secretary. The outward trappings of commercial success do not interest her in the same way that they appeal to men. For a man, the huge car and big house tend to be extensions of himself, proofs that he exists and is successful. The average woman in business is much keener to make a good product, balance her books and get on with the job. She does not have to be seen in smart restaurants, and is unlikely to be interested in acquiring a cellar full of fine wines, or antiques just for show.

It is true that you will not very often find women heading such big businesses as Marks and Spencer, Heron, or EMI. In starting up their own concerns, men often go for the big killing, whereas women tend to be more content with a much smaller canvas. In business, women do not usually want to conquer the whole world, but just want to run their own little patch honestly and profitably.

If you are considering starting up your own business, you first of all need to ask yourself what you would be happiest doing. The most successful businesses tend to be those built on existing skills, rather than attempts at venturing into an unknown area. So if you have worked in computers for a number of years, it makes sense to think about a business in the computer area. Then, you need to know whether there would be a market for what you intend to produce. Some preliminary market research is essential – it's no good just hoping for the best. There has to be some good reason why people would buy your product; either because it's cheaper, or because you offer a service or commodity not otherwise easily obtainable.

In some cases you may have to create a market where there was none before. I'm thinking here of two modern examples: selling art prints to offices, and timeshare holidays. Both of these are relatively new concepts for the British public, so a considerable effort has to be put into marketing at the outset.

Then, having established that there is a market available, and it's not one that will readily dry up, you need to know whether you would be happy doing your own thing. Running a one-woman business can be very lonely, and it would probably not be profitable at first. Even if you are a ready market, and your product is first class, you will still have to put a lot of effort into persuading people to buy. This can mean working far longer hours than you would for anybody else. Don't start up a business if you only want a little part-time job – much dedication is needed for success.

But women are in fact, extraordinarily good at selling. It's something they have at last woken up to in America, where large firms are employing more and more women in the sales force. Women are good at selling because, far more than men, they pick up the unspoken signals from potential customers. That famous female intuition, which is a reality, is a great asset in the business world.

In selling, a woman very much has a head start over a man. A woman's voice, in the first place, tends to be more attractive and appealing, less threatening. The boss of a telephone answering company told me once that people are far more likely to leave messages when they hear a woman's voice, than when a gruff male voice answers. People are also less likely to shut their doors in the face of an attractive-looking woman than they are with a man. Women are less frightening, generally, than men, and they can more easily get an 'in' to companies.

In companies where aggressive selling is very much part of the business, you will nearly always find that women are employed as telephone salespersons. Somehow, they come over as more honest and sincere than a man. A woman can be quietly insistent, whereas a man will often become loud and strident.

Also, women's faces and figures are, generally speaking, pleasanter to look at than a man's. That's why pretty female faces are usually found on the covers of magazines. If male faces sold more copies, they'd have these instead. The aesthetic appeal should not, in business, be dismissed as frivolous. Men still tend to wonder that an attractive-looking female can be sitting there and trying to sell them something. While they're still wondering, they will have ordered a dozen of what the lady is selling.

In my profession, journalism, I have a feeling that women can be more successful when they set up on their own. Certainly, there are some very successful women freelance journalists around, and it's not hard to see how they got where they are.

Women, generally, have a greater capacity for hard work than men, and more than that, they can think of several different things at once. Nearly all of the career women I know can do their jobs, get the lunch, remember their mother-in-law's birthday, and still get through more work than a man who never stops to think about anything else. A man very much tends to give his all to the job in hand, but this doesn't necessarily make him more efficient!

Women also tend to be better at looking after their employees. Once a man hires staff, he takes the attitude that they are there to do a job of work, and he would not be interested in whether they had boyfriend problems, or whether a young man was going through a divorce. His feeling would be, that they are being paid to do a job, and it's not his concern what their private lives are like. But when a woman hires staff, she will know every little detail about them, and is actually interested in what makes them tick. Some women used to feel that they would not like working for a woman boss, but thankfully, this is changing, and many women running their businesses and employing an all-female staff have been happily coexisting for years. There tends to be a higher turnover of staff in a basically male company.

Women are less liable than men to fiddle their income tax returns, or to make false claims about what they are selling. Nearly all the businesswomen I interviewed make a practice of being scrupulously honest, whereas a man can feel he is being rather 'wet' if he doesn't fiddle the system somehow, and use it to his own advantage.

The qualities needed for success in your own business are, I think, first and foremost, that you have to be jolly good at what you are doing. If you think you would like to go into business handknitting jumpers, these must be of topmost quality. Your customers should not be able to get something better than you can produce, at a cheaper price.

Secondly, you must know that you can sell your product. This means spending quite a lot of time before actually setting up, researching the possibilities. Could you sell enough of your product in the area where you live? If not, why not?

Then, you need to work out the money side. How much will it cost you to set up: do you need capital equipment, do you have to rent premises or employ staff? It is far better, with any business, to set up very modestly, and then expand as you go. Before deciding to rent expensive office space, see if you can carry on the business in your home first.

Almost any business, however modest, costs money to set up. It is quite easy to go to the bank with your business proposal and ask to borrow a sum of money. Very many people indeed set up businesses like this, and banks have departments which are specially geared to help small businesses get off the ground. But you also have to bear in mind that banks are not philanthropic organizations, and lend you money only because you will be paying it back at a rate of interest. So, again, you will have to work out how much your first year's turnover will have to be before you can break even.

You must, at the outset, have some idea of the kind of money you intend to make, and whether the business you are envisaging will yield the return you would like. If you are thinking about starting a labour-intensive business, such as producing exclusive handknits, you will have to take into account that each garment will take a long time to complete. If you are not careful, you could find yourself earning about 50 pence an hour, literally. Then, can you get your raw materials at cost, or would you have to pay the full retail price?

Would you want to work so hard for so little money? Almost any craft product, unless it can be mass-produced in some way, takes a lot of time and trouble to achieve. You have to be able to mass-produce in order to make a fortune, or else charge a fortune. A couturier gown can cost several thousand pounds but most designers make their real money from their ready-to-wear, mass-produced collections and accessories.

You have to work out how much money you need to make a week in order to get by, and pay your bills. Calculations will have to be done on how much of your weekly turnover will go towards the rent, heating, lighting, raw materials, travel, wages. The next task is to work out how this amount is to be realized. It is never possible to forecast exactly, of course, but if you have a fairly precise sum in mind, it's marvellous how close you find yourself coming to this target. You have to say to yourself: I must sell at least 300 a week of these to make £250, of which half will be profit.

You must, of course, set yourself realistic targets. If you are in the business of handpainting eggs, it is unlikely that you will make a million of them in your first year. But if you set up a company producing match box stickers or cereal packet toys, you will be thinking in terms of large numbers.

Ask yourself also whether you intend to do most of the work yourself, or employ others at the outset. Though you may decide not to pay yourself a living wage for a year, say, you can't inflict this on employees, who will want to be paid at the end of the week whether you have the money in the till or not. Very generally speaking, it is best not to take on any staff until you can be reasonably sure your weekly takings will pay their wages plus a little bit over.

You must have a very clear idea of how hard you are prepared to work. Suppose you have three children under five and no help in the house, you may only want to work in the evenings and at weekends. In this case, it will take a long time to make a fortune, or even a living wage.

Whatever you decide to sell – and all businesses involve selling something – you must believe in yourself, and your ability to market whatever you have decided to produce or offer. Would you be prepared to get on the telephone and try to interest someone you don't know in taking 500 of your wooden egg cups? Or does the thought make you quake and shake at the knees? Few fortunes are made by starting a shop and hoping people will come in and buy. Somehow, you have to attract them, by selling something different, being open at unusual hours, or offering a much-needed service. You have to alert people to the fact that you exist, and this may mean taking ads in local papers, having huge signs, having leaflets printed, or otherwise advertising your wares. The world can only beat a pathway to your door once it knows you are there.

One golden rule in business, I think, is to make sure you execute your orders in exactly the manner that you promise. Suppose you are setting up as an interior decorator, and say you will come and give an estimate on Friday at 3 p.m. You must turn up on Friday at 3 p.m., whatever happens, particularly if you are dealing with a new client.

One of the least attractive aspects of business life, for many people, is the keeping of the books. I hate this job myself, but it must be done, and it is vital to keep books accurate and up-to-date. As soon as you receive an order, write it down in a special order book, and send out your invoices regularly every month.

You must be able to ask people for the money they owe you. You will very rapidly find out, once you set up in business, that nobody is ever in a hurry to pay. So you must make your terms very, very clear at the start. If you need money in advance for materials, say so, and get it before you start on the order. This is usual for many building and decorating jobs. If you must have a deposit, insist on this being paid before you start on the job.

Some people, especially young ones, are so anxious when they start up in business and so desperate for orders, that they waive the deposit and are slow at sending out invoices. But you must overcome this reluctance and remember that everybody prefers to deal with somebody who is behaving professionally. If you make an estimate for your piece of work, and then find you have wildly underestimated, then I'm afraid it is up to you to bear the cost of your mistake, and vow never to make it again.

Everybody does make mistakes in business, but the clever ones learn by them. Never, ever, underquote to gain an order, and then put up your original estimate. You may get your money, but you certainly won't win friends and influence people, and very many businesses indeed proceed by word of mouth recommendation.

If you doubt your competence to carry out a particular piece of work, then don't undertake it. No one is going to thank you for doing a shoddy job. Many people think they would like to turn a hobby into a profitable business, and indeed, this is being done very successfully all the time. But you must remember that, once you are in business, time is money. For example, I enjoy giving dinner parties and cooking nice dishes, but I would hate to do this for a living, as then I would have to be cost-effective.

Also important, if you are thinking about marketing a particular product, is to know which section of the market you intend to aim at. Is it to be the top end, or are you going for mass appeal? It is very unlikely that the same commodity would appeal to every sector. Suppose you want to produce beautiful hand-smocked dresses for children. These will probably not be successful in working-class communities, where mothers may be far more concerned about whether they can bung them in the washing machine. Only rich people will be prepared to pay the prices and admire the workmanship or, alternatively, tourists to the country may provide a market.

Here are some stories of women who have set up their own businesses. All the stories are very different indeed but they give an idea of what can be done.

Debbie Moore, managing director of Pineapple Dance Studios, had the bright idea of setting up her own dance class business. A former model, she had left school at 15, with no academic qualifications. She is now in her mid-thirties, married for the second time, and has a daughter. In 1979 she borrowed £30,000 from her bank manager and opened up a dance studio in a former pineapple warehouse in Covent Garden. Three year later, her company went public, and now has branches in Manchester and New York. She says the secret of her success is an ability to communicate with people, and to gather round herself a wonderful team of helpers.

'You have to be able to do that famous word, "delegate",' she was quoted as saying when she won the Businesswoman of the Year title in 1984. I feel that the secret of her success lay in knowing, somehow, that a big boom in health and fitness was about to start, and getting in at the start. Also, the dance studio she had previously been attending herself closed down temporarily and many teachers were left without anywhere to go and teach.

The Pineapple Studios are a first-class example of how to get in at the very start of a trend. The enterprise was undoubtedly helped by Debbie's appearance – she looks like all those attending her studios would like to look. (This aspect also partly explains Jane Fonda's success with a similar venture in America. If you are going to deal in a commodity where looks are important, it helps to have those looks yourself. I don't imagine that a balding, cigar-smoking, paunchy middle-aged man would have had anything like the success that Debbie Moore has had.) If you are pretty and/or glamorous, it doesn't hurt to make full use of these qualities.

Margaret Theroux is the main brains behind the First Computer, a new chain of high street shops selling computers to small businesses. She had an idea that it was time to have high street shops selling these, and put together a business package. American by birth, she had worked in computers in America for many years. She persuaded big businessmen to invest around two million pounds in her First Computer shops. She said she had always seen herself as a businesswoman. Maggie is married to a management consultant and has two small daughters. She epitomizes one of the first rules about business: there has to be a large potential market for what you are going to sell if you are to hit the big time.

Jean Morgan-Bryant exports construction machinery to the United Arab Emirates and recently her exports exceeded three million pounds, winning her a Smaller Business Export award. Jean started in business life 15 years ago typing letters for a small plant and export company in London. Ten years later she was a director of the firm, which closed down in 1978. She started Morgan-Bryant Marketing with her savings, and set out to conquer the Gulf, asking for contracts. She spoke hardly a word of Arabic, but she obtained her contracts nonetheless.

Ruth van Ruyckevelt received a substantial order from Harrods, less than a month after starting her own glass engraving business. Ruth had put herself on a glass technology course sponsored by the Manpower Services Commission, with a view to setting up her own business in this area.

Beth Chatto developed a love of gardening while she was at home bringing up her family. She now specializes in growing and selling unusual plants. Here is her story: 'Between leaving college and taking up a career as a teacher, I married Andrew Chatto, who was a fruit grower in my home village. I became a founder member of our own local Flower Club, and before long was invited to do demonstrations of flower arranging. I quickly realized what a great need there was for a nursery producing unusual plants.

'At that time, happily engaged in bringing up my young daughters, helping my husband to run the fruit farm, and together both enjoying our joint hobby of gardening, it never occurred to me that I might one day be faced with the necessity of turning it into a business. However, my husband's health was deteriorating, and we made the decision that the farm should go.' Beth then decided to start up her own nursery specializing in unusual plants and now has 12 acres under cultivation at Elmstead Market, near Colchester, and a staff of between 14 and 20 people.

She says: 'Many visitors from all parts of the world come to visit famous English gardens, and among them now they come to visit mine. I must confess I do feel a little glow of pride that they do seek my garden, which 20 years ago was a wilderness, and which could revert to a wilderness again.'

Beth passes on this advice to potential businesswomen: 'I think it is being obliged to exploit your abilities which is important. You are obviously going to be much happier and make a much more successful life for yourself if you are putting your whole life and soul into something you like doing.'

For examples of women who have been outstandingly successful in business, you only have to look at the cosmetics industry. There was Helena Rubinstein, Elizabeth Arden and, nearer our own times, Mary Quant and Estée Lauder.

But a business does not have to worldwide to be successful. In almost every small town there are women running very profitable little businesses, as hairdressers, beauty therapists, private nurses, shopkeepers, dressmakers, typists, accountants and solicitors. The global operation is not for everybody, and everyone who has read biographies of Miss Rubinstein and Miss Arden will realize that they were not the pleasantest of people to have around.

Though women tend to be nicer in business, this is not always the case and, if they choose, they can be very ruthless operators indeed. When Elizabeth Arden divorced her husband, she made him sign a five-year contract not to work for any rival cosmetic company. The day his contract was up, Helena Rubinstein contacted him. She announced: 'He comes to work for me.'

Both these women were quite ruthless, and set up their empires at the expense of shattered personal lives, and attempts to destroy their rival's reputations. Women *can* be like this, and it is interesting to speculate on what made Arden and Rubinstein such driven, unlikeable people. But most women in business aren't even remotely like these two cosmetic queens.

Here are some brief examples of women who have set themselves up in business on a modest, but nevertheless successful, scale. Ros Tarrant designs and knits personalized knitwear, for stars as well as ordinary people. Joanna Vignola specializes in patchwork items, and has had a stall at Covent Garden in London. Sue Rodgers started up the Mayfield Cat Boarding Establishment in Kent. Sue describes how she set up her cattery:

'When I mentioned to my vet that I wanted to make some money working from home, he immediately suggested a cattery, which was very much needed in the area where I live. As our house already had a stable block, the room was there. I had to apply to the local council for a change of use to the property, and submit plans for the cattery. These were approved, and the next step was to get a bank loan to get the enterprise off the ground.

'But before getting any money together, I went round to all the neighbours, told them what I proposed doing, and asked whether they had any objections. None had, so I then began to go ahead with designing cat runs.

'A friend helped me there. I wanted each cat to have a bedroom and its own run. These cost £350 each to design and build, and my vet came along to inspect them. He thought they were super, as did the Cat Protection League warden. My next job was to advertise in local papers and in vets' surgeries.

'I've found it pays to be very organized right from the start. You have to be licensed to run a cattery or kennels, and I thought it would be a good idea to keep proper account books and have an accountant. You learn that you can set items like the car, and some domestic bills, against tax.'

Sue feels that a cattery is an ideal job for a mother at home – she has a young son – but she says you must genuinely love animals. 'Also, the market has to be there, and you have to enjoy what you are doing. When the cats come back, they remember you, and become friends. That is the real satisfaction of the work.' Sue says she does not make exactly a fortune, but can expand or contract any time she likes. When she goes on holiday herself, she closes the cattery down. Otherwise, when it is full, she estimates that it takes about two hours a day to maintain.

It is a very good idea, whatever line of business you intend to be in, to retain the services of an accountant. She (or he) will explain all you need to know about tax and book-keeping. Then you should find out whether you need to register your company, how to organize cash flow, whether you need a trade name, or to set yourself up as a limited company, and how your business is going to come to you. Your local bank's Small Business Unit will explain all the legal implications, and your accountant will also put you right.

If setting up on your own, you will want the Inland Revenue to treat you as a self-employed person, otherwise you could find yourself having to pay PAYE, which means that you have your income tax deducted at source. Usually, being self-employed means that you work in your own premises, rather than those of your clients, though you may be required to go there on occasion. If you work all the time at your client's address, you may find yourself being regarded by the tax inspector as an employee.

So, before starting, make sure you understand the difference between being employed and being self-employed. If you sign a contract with a firm, this could lead to your being treated as an employee. You must not assume that the people who use your services, or buy your products, will themselves know their way round the Inland Revenue jungle. It is your business, not theirs, to find out, and make sure you know all the snags and benefits.

As a general principle, charge by the job rather than by the hour or week. Most self-employed people do work on this basis, though it may not apply if you are running a cattery, for example.

You do not need to have a special trade name before you can set up in business, but it is a good idea to have printed business letter headings. You can, within limits, call yourself anything you like, so long as you are not infringing anyone else's trade name, or calling yourself something that can lead to misinterpretation. For example, if you are running a riding school, it may be misleading to call yourself The Queen's Royal Stables. In fact, calling yourself 'royal' anything could give the impression that you have a royal warrant, and this could get you into trouble. (Unless, of course, you actually *have* a royal warrant.)

Those who decide to trade under their own names, such as Jane Smith, do not need to register a trade name. But if you are calling yourself Acme Typewriter Services, or Supercuddle Toys, then you must register with the registrar of business names. There are three main registries for this and their addresses are:

For England: Pembroke House, 40-65 City Road, London EC1 2DN
For Scotland: 102 George Street, Edinburgh
For Northern Ireland: 43-47 Chichester Street, Belfast

The Registry will be able to send you the Department of Trade's pamphlet, *Notes for Guidance on Registration of Business Names*. Never go to the expense of having stationery printed before you are sure that the business name you have in mind is all right to use.

The next big hurdle to overcome is deciding on your accounting year. Actually, it's not so horrendous as it seems at first, if you have a good accountant to advise you. Your best choice of accountant is somebody who understands and handles small businesses, so that he can advise you on maximum tax advantage. There are many ways round the tax system if you are self-employed, and many of these are decidedly advantageous. You do not, for instance, have to pay your tax as soon as you earn the money.

You pay it in a lump sum, usually twice a year, in January and July, and this can be up to two years in arrears, so long as certain conditions are met. This delay is not always an advantage, and can work against you if you unexpectedly have a bad year. Self-employed tax is usually worked out on the basis that you can earn a bit more each year. If a business is running as it should, this will be the case.

You often read stories of actors being asked by the Inland Revenue to pay huge back-dated sums of tax that, usually, they don't have. This happens when their tax, like most self-employed people's, is worked out on an arrears basis, and they are 'resting' at the time the demand is due. If they had an exceptionally good year two years previously, and spent it all, they can be in real trouble. The moral of this is, always have enough money to pay your tax, in a separate, sacrosanct account, not a current one that you can raid at any time. Tax for self-employed people can be a constant worry, unless you plan for it carefully in advance.

Always have separate accounts for business and personal use, otherwise huge muddles will inevitably result. Have a separate paying-in book, too, for all the cheques that come to you, and carefully store your bank statements, in numerical order. Your accountant will need to have these at the end of each financial year which, for self-employed people, usually comes at the end of April.

It is probably best, at the outset, not to take too much notice of friends and relatives' advice, however well meaning. Instead, get objective third party advice from your local Small Firms Centre, which are run by the Department of Industry. These centres are marvellous for anybody who is contemplating setting up on their own, and as they don't cost anything, you might as well take advantage of them, and pick their brains. The centres are run, not by civil servants, who may know little about the practicalities of setting up a business, but former business people who have been through it all themselves.

To find your nearest branch, dial 100 and then ask for Freefone 2444. A consultation can help you avoid many of the obvious pitfalls, and work out whether your plans are realistic enough. You do not have to abide by the advice you are given, but you can hear it, and then digest it. The Shell Small Business Unit have a number of 10-minute films that are available on free loan to groups, and these give success stories of people who have set up in business on their own. Several of these are women. Further details from: The Shell Film Library, 25 The Burroughs, Hendon, London NW2 4AT (01-202 7803). The films are available on free loan on 16mm, VHS or U-Matic Video cassette. They tell you how some enterprising people have made a job out of a hobby, or former spare-time interest. Beth Chatto, whose story was mentioned earlier in the chapter, is one of the participants in the Shell films.

Also, many colleges round the country run short courses on how to keep books, how to manage tax, and how to go about working for yourself. The attractions of attending an initial course on self-employment – particularly if the idea of a home-based business is new to you – is that you soon meet other people who are in the same position as yourself.

Before buying any equipment, work out whether you really need it, and whether you could manage without it. Every item you buy must be able to pay its way, and actually add to your profitability or efficiency. That being said, you do need to look professional right from the start, so make sure you have business cards printed. This is a good investment, as you will find that, as soon as you set up in business, people are always asking for your card.

The style of printing should be one that you feel accurately reflects the service or product you are offering. A quick flip through the catalogue of any good quality printing works will give you an idea of the kind of thing on offer. While you are at it, have plenty printed up, as they are expensive in small quantities, and should last you years.

It sounds obvious, but buy envelopes, paper, paperclips, or anything else you are likely to need in quantity, in bulk. It's a real bore having to go out to shops to buy little packets of envelopes or rubber bands. If you use the typewriter a lot, buy your ribbons in bulk as well. You will soon find that, when you are running your own business, any time you save is money saved as well. Buy ball point pens by the gross, if you use them a lot.

When I first set myself up as a freelance writer, I knew I would need a filing cabinet. Actually, this is an essential piece of equipment for any business whatsoever, so do invest in one right away. I could have bought a cheap, second-hand grey cabinet, which would have done the job just as well, but I was self-indulgent and bought instead, a new, expensive, emerald green one. My excuse was that, as I was going to sit looking at the cabinet every day for years on end, I might as well get one that wasn't too much of an eyesore. Seven years later, the cabinet is still as good as new, and I find I use it every single day.

I also knew that I would need a telephone answering machine, a good quality typewriter and a comfortable chair, as I didn't want my earning capacity to be cut short by excruciating backache. Generally speaking, it is worth getting the best quality equipment you can afford, if you will be using it on a daily basis. You don't want to have to replace items like typewriters, or filing cabinets too often. But I didn't spend money on a desk. Instead, I bought a very cheap dining table, costing £12, and varnished it dark brown. Since it is usually covered with paper and files, there was little point in purchasing an expensive leather-topped desk that would soon be ruined. The dining table has served me as well as any desk could, and gives me far more working space than an average-sized one.

As time went on, I acquired a photocopying machine and electronic typewriter with memory. The other essential piece of equipment was a calculator.

I found it was better to acquire capital items gradually, rather than buy them all at once, as you then get a better idea of what you really need. You cannot expect to know this all at the start.

I knew that, for me, there was no advantage in having a prestige office suite in the middle of London, a secretary, or a flash car. None of these would have helped in the slightest to make me more successful. By contrast, Maggie Theroux, of First Computer, knew that West End offices were essential for her business, as was a secretary. But she didn't, either, need a smart car. It all depends on the type of business you are envisaging.

An essential part of any business operation is claiming expenses to set against tax. My advice is no fiddling here, as it makes life too uncomfortable, and a person who is not quite honest is always a pain, rather than a pleasure, to do business with. Claiming expenses, an absolute essential in any business operation, involves keeping a careful note of everything you spend that pertains to the business, and all receipts. At first, you may not know exactly what you are entitled to claim, so keep all receipts in case. Everybody has their own pet method, but the one that works for me is to throw everything relating to VAT in one envelope, and all receipts that accompany cheques into a big box. Then I have a huge sort out once a month or so. All receipts, whether or not they are VAT-related, go into the VAT envelope, so that they can be kept in the one place. They are all useful for the accountant. All my cheque stubs, bank statements and credit card transactions are kept in a separate drawer.

A separate file contains all the bills I have to pay, such as telephone, television licence, VAT, and is labelled: Bills to be paid.

I also have a big red book, provided by my accountant, wherein is entered all my orders, gross payment (including VAT), net payment, date of payment and the publication which ordered the article. In another part of the book are kept all my expenses, petrol, travel, stationery, and so on. The main purpose of this book is to simplify life for my accountant and the advantage for the businesswoman is that it helps to keep the accountant's own bills down.

At first, I kept forgetting to ask for petrol receipts, or to keep the little slips you get at stationers. But I soon got into the habit, and it is now automatic. It is very important that it does, because otherwise you soon get into a hopeless muddle. I used to be extremely bad at maths but, since running my own business, I find I have improved out of all recognition. When it's a matter of your own livelihood, you find your abilities sharpen up in all sorts of important directions.

What can you claim for? This depends very much on the nature of your business. Some people can claim for special clothes, if these have to be worn for work. This can be a highly contentious issue, as in the case of barrister Ann Mallalieu, who claimed that the black and white clothes she had to wear for her work were not the kind of outfits she would otherwise have chosen. If you have to buy special overalls, or other protective gear, you will almost certainly be entitled to claim for these, as you will for cleaning bills.

Your accountant's fees are tax deductible, and he will advise on what you can set against tax. Some people can claim for their TV licence, and for a video recorder. Others can't, but may instead be able to claim for a special sewing machine, or footwear for instance.

As a general guide, you can set against tax the following: telephone, any advertising, cleaning, stationery, heating and lighting. Be careful about rent, rates and mortgage, as you could find yourself lumbered for capital gains tax when you sell your house. Again, your accountant should know the way round all these mazes – after all, they deal with this sort of thing all the time.

Wages and salaries of any staff you employ directly in the business are also allowable. This means you can claim for a secretary or messenger but not, if you are a woman, a childminder or domestic help. There has been much to-ing and fro-ing about this, but nothing has changed yet. If you want your childminder to be listed as a secretary, you will have to show that she does mainly secretarial work. This can be dodgy. Men can claim for domestic help on their tax forms if they are single parents, but women are not equal in this respect, as yet.

A word about taking on staff: don't take anybody on unless you know for sure you can pay their wages. If it is going to be a constant worry, do it all yourself until you are better established. You don't want all your hard-earned profit draining out on wages. Use an answering machine rather than getting somebody in to sit there answering the phone. Obviously, the latter is nicer, but will it gain you extra business?

Employees can easily become a major headache, particularly in the early days of running a business, when cash flow might be slow. One of the more problematic aspects of running your own business is that money does not always come in just when you need it. Unlike a regular salary cheque, it can be months and months before you see what you earn being stashed away in the bank. Before you employ anybody at all, do get leaflet NP 15 from the Social Security office and read it carefully. It explains National Insurance Contributions which you will have to pay if you employ people for more than a certain number of hours per week.

One of the iniquities of a home business is that, when a wife works for her husband, her earned income can be set against tax, but if a wife employs a husband, no extra tax can be claimed. The Inland Revenue are all male chauvinists, and work on the assumption that a married woman is financially dependent on her husband, even when she isn't.

Anybody who works part-time, that is less than 16 hours a week, is exempt from PAYE and National Insurance, so it may be worth your while to have a succession of part-time people, or use them on a freelance basis, when they can worry about their own tax and insurance. The question to ask yourself before employing anybody is: will they make me money over and above the extra bother and paperwork they cause? Will they reduce, or add to, my headaches? If you can manage without staff, it is better to go it alone. There is plenty of time to consider employing people once your business has expanded. If you are setting up a retail shop, however, it will be almost essential to have help right from the start, otherwise you may find you can't even go to the loo or the bank.

You will be able to claim tax relief on bank charges, or money to borrow to buy essential equipment. Insurance taken out for the business, subscriptions to trade and professional organisations and journals, travel and hotel bills incurred in the course of your business, entertaining for overseas, though not for home clients, bad debts, depreciation on capital goods such as a car or a computer, are all allowed. To help you further through all this, you can get leaflet IR 28, *Starting in Business*, from your nearest Tax Office. It really is worth doing your homework and reading through all these leaflets before starting up, as you will certainly have to cope with all the aspects listed, even if you envisage running only a very small business. It always pays to be businesslike.

National Insurance Contributions are a must for anybody in business on their own. You will be paying Class Two contributions at £4.60 a week, unless your earnings total less than £1,850 a year (1985 levels). The leaflet NI 41, *National Insurance Contributions for the Self Employed*, gives you all the current gen. These Class Two contributions entitle you to a state pension, sickness and invalid benefit, basic maternity and widow's allowance. If your business suddenly picks up, and you make between £4,000 and £13,000 a year profit, you will also have to pay Class Four contributions, for which there is no perceptible benefit at all. The ceiling of £13,000 applies, however much more than that you may make, and you still have to pay only 6.3 per cent of this amount.

If you have been out of work you can ask at your local Job Centre about the Enterprise Allowance, worth £40 a week, and specifically intended for those starting up their own businesses. To qualify, you must be at least 18, or under 60, and able to contribute £1,000 capital of your own. This can come from savings, a legacy, or even a bank loan.

Taxation for married women is a subject that has vexed many would-be liberated women for many years. Even today, the money you earn on your own account goes onto your husband's tax demand, unless you specifically elect, every year, to have a form of your own. It is one of the continuing daftnesses of the Inland Revenue (and there are many) and does not look like changing in the near future. All the combined anger, pressure groups and demands of the married women I know to have the system altered, has so far fallen on completely deaf ears. Unless you make a special, annual effort to be taxed separately, you will find your earnings are considered, for tax purposes, to be your husband's. This applies even if you are the major breadwinner of your family. It is unfair and iniquitous, but still it goes on, and as yet there does not seem to be even a glimmer of change on the horizon.

At the moment, as a wife, you can earn £2005 a year before paying any tax. If you and your husband between you are earning £24,000 or more, then you can elect to have your tax separately assessed. Below this amount, it is simply not worth it, unless you are intent on proving a point. There is actually a tax disadvantage, as the husband then loses his married man's allowance, and gets the lower single person's allowance instead. But the wife gains by having her personal earnings taxed at 30 per cent, instead of being tagged onto her husband's income, and therefore taxed at the higher rate. More details of this anachronistic horror can be found in the Inland Revenue leaflet IR IS: *Income Tax: Wife's Earnings Election*.

Franchising

One increasingly popular way to set up in business is to run a franchise operation. Franchises, though initially frowned on by the British, are now a feature of every high street, and they have been phenomenally successful over the past few years. Examples are: Wimpy Bars, Spud-U-Like, British School of Motoring, Holland and Barrett health shops (some), Body Shops, Kall-Kwik print shops, Budget Rent-a-Car, and Yves Rocher beauty shops. The idea is that you buy your way into a business that is already well established. Disadvantages are that you must run your outlet in exactly the same way as all the others: there is little, if any scope, for individual flair.

Many fast food outlets are now franchises, and the concept is half way between being a manager and running your own show completely. You will have to pay from around £5,000 for a franchise to sell a product, or offer a service, in a certain area. You should look for the opportunity to sell something that has already been tried and tested, and a firm that provides good initial training and back-up facilities. You will gain from the national advertising, and having experts on tap to advise you. Before going ahead with any particular franchise, check that they have a good reputation, and that their business is run on reputable lines.

You should also find out just what the initial fee covers, and your likely turnover within the next few years. If it all sounds vague, or can't yield enough for your needs, forget the idea.

It is important to interview other established franchises who are already in the operation you are considering. Here, don't just go for the tame ones recommended by the franchisor, but seek out your own people. Make sure that both a solicitor and an accountant look over the proposals before you let yourself in for signing anything.

Make sure you take on a franchise that is a member of the British Franchise Association. This professional body ensures that all its members have been running their business for at least two years, successfully, before it will accept any new people for membership.

Running a franchise is not an automatic passport to business success, nor is it a means of succeeding in business without really trying. You will have to work hard to establish your outlet, and certainly put far more hours in than you would as an employee. It is still up to you to make sure the business is profitable, and grows every year. Though it is said that around 80 per cent of franchises are successful – the same percentage of other businesses go bust – there are some catastrophic failures, and these are happening all the time. As a franchisee, you will have very little legal protection if the parent company does go bankrupt, and you will usually have lost a lot of money.

Banks, though, have now become converted to the idea of franchises, and borrowing money to start up your operation should not be a problem. Most franchisors are now very keen to attract women as they have come to believe that females make ideal franchisees. They are prepared to work hard, but are less likely than men to want to get their own bright idea off the ground. At least, that's how the thinking goes.

If the idea attracts you, do take a look at this newish way of starting up in business. There is more to franchising than running a Dyno-Rod or Kentucky Fried Chicken. *Colour Counsellors*, for example, is an all-female interior decorating franchise started up by Virginia Stourton. Franchisees get eight boxes, all containing swatches of furnishing fabrics, so that clients can be advised on how to make their homes colour co-ordinated. This operation, which is very successful indeed, now has a long waiting list of people wanting to join. But as one franchise of 13 years told me, you can't just buy the franchise and suddenly expect business to come to you. You still have to go out and get it, and it is no use trying to start up in an area where people don't want advice on how best to furnish their homes.

For preliminary advice on starting up a Franchise business, contact: *The British Franchise Association*, Grove House, Colnbrook, Slough S13 QH (01-964 4909).

VAT

If your turnover – not profit – is more than £19,500 (1985 figures), you will, by law, have to register for VAT. This tax, bugbear of so many small businesses, is a legal requirement, and once you get used to it, it's not so bad as it first appears. If your VAT is very complicated, it is probably best to ask your accountant to handle it for you, bearing in mind, of course, that he will make an extra charge for carrying out this work.

What happens is that, once you know your annual income is likely to exceed the VAT lower limit, you contact your local VAT office. Their number will be in your phone book. They will send round a VAT inspector who will sit with you and patiently explain how you should keep your books, what you can claim for, and how you should send out your invoices.

The VAT person will stay with you until she is certain you have understood all the intricacies. She may then later make a surprise call on you and ask to inspect your books at any time. In theory, a self-employed business person should benefit from VAT, as you can claim on many items, such as capital goods, petrol and telephone bills.

Once you are registered for VAT, you will be given a number, and you must then charge 15 per cent VAT on all your bills. This can look as though you are earning more than you actually are, so you must make sure that you mentally deduct 15 per cent from every cheque you receive. Every quarter, in March, June, September and December, you will have to pay the VAT back to the Customs and Excise Office in Southend. They are very strict about it, too. You do have a month's grace to pay the VAT, but must send it out not later than a month after it becomes due. There is no possible way to delay paying the VAT, so make sure you always have enough money in your business account to cover this.

I think that it can look good to be registered for VAT, as this makes you immediately seem professional and successful. But if your annual turnover goes much below the current £19,500 limit (which is always liable to change slightly at Budget time in March), you may be asked to de-register. Just about any retail outlet, however small, should have a turnover of £19,500 or more, but this may not apply to typing services, making cuddly toys, handsmocking dresses or making peasant jewellery. To be registered for VAT is in itself a small sign of success, though it is rather a nuisance in reality.

Checklist of questions to ask yourself before setting up in business:

1. Do I have enough marketable skills in a particular area to be reasonably certain I can make a go of my own business?

2 Would I enjoy working alone, and not having the security of a monthly paycheque?

3 Could I cope with rejection, if nobody wanted my work at first?

4 Could I persuade people to buy what I sell?

5 Do I want to be a successful businesswoman?

6 Will I be able to keep books, accounts and cash flow moving properly?

If the answer to all these is yes – well, what's stopping you?

Further Reading and Information

Earning Money at Home (The Consumers' Association, 1980).

A Woman in Your Own Right, Ann Dickson (Quartet Books, 1983).

How to Survive Unemployment, Robert Nathan and Michael Syrett (Penguin, 1983).

Stress and the Woman Manager, Professor Cary Cooper and Dr Marilyn Davidson (Oxford, 1983).

Creating Your Own Work, Micheline Mason (Gresham Books, 1983).

Work For Yourself: A Guide For Young People, Paddy Hall (National Extension College, 1983).

Information and help on setting up a business:

National Federation of Self Employed and Small Businesses, Ltd., 45 Russell Square, London WC1

Council for Small Industries in Rural Areas, 141 Castle Street, Salisbury, Wilts.

The Crafts Council, 12 Waterloo Place, London SW1Y 4AU (they publish a booklet, 'Setting Up a Workshop', which is helpful for anybody thinking about starting a crafts business).

7

Your Rights At Work

All too many women are so grateful to have a job – any job – that they never even bother to find out what their rights are. But it's certainly worth taking the trouble to discover your legal position, as there are now many, many rights to protect workers. It's up to you to be aware of these, as employers are unlikely to go out of their way to point these out to you.

If you work part-time – that is, eight hours a week or less – you are not entitled to any employment protection whatsoever. Part-time workers who put in between eight and sixteen hours a week gain some limited protection, and this increases with length of service. But to benefit from the maximum statutory rights, you need to be working full-time, which is defined as 16 hours a week or more for the same employer.

In the bad old days, employees could be sacked without pay at a minute's notice, and had no legal redress. Those days have now thankfully disappeared, and successive Acts of Parliament have made it even more difficult to dislodge the willing worker from her place of employment. As far as women are concerned, the Equal Pay Act of 1970 and the Sex Discrimination Act of 1975 have made life a little more tolerable in the workplace, though these pieces of legislation have by no means removed all of the iniquities.

In theory, you are entitled to the same as a man for 'broadly similar work'. This means that if your job description is identical to that of a male worker, you cannot be paid less than him. But as we have seen, women do still earn very much less than men, and I doubt that the Equal Pay Act has made very much difference to this. In Britain, women earn on average 69 per cent of male earnings, and in a nationwide survey undertaken by the Office of Population, Census and Surveys, it was found that only 15 per cent of women earned as much as, or more than, their husbands.

The term 'broadly similar' can hide a multitude of sins. Though men and women must be paid for the same jobs, we find that it is nearly all men in the higher reaches of any profession. So it is unlikely, in many instances, that many of the jobs would be seen as broadly similar. If you find that you are being paid less than a man doing an identical job, with identical training and background, then you would have a case against your company. But before becoming indignant at this injustice, you would have to check whether the man had been there longer, or whether he came with higher, or different, qualifications. His job description might also carry an 'X' factor, meaning that, as a man, he might be asked to do a job that could not be demanded of a woman.

This would not be the case in many jobs, perhaps, but it can happen. For example, in the Armed Forces, women officers are paid on the same scale as male officers, apart from this 'X' factor, which, in service terms means willingness to go to war. At the moment, women are not asked to fight, though they may be needed with back-up and auxiliary aid. A man's job description, in other professions or occupations, may include night shift work, which would not be expected of a woman, or involve the possibility of working in Saudi Arabia, where women are forbidden to work on equal terms with men.

If you feel you have got a case, the next step is to seek the advice of the Equal Opportunities Commission. They are well used to handling equal pay disputes, and can tell you whether you are justified in pursuing your grievance. It's not unknown for firms to write out different job descriptions for men and women, just so that they can pay the men more, or the women less, depending on which way you want to look at it.

Whenever you land a job, you must make doubly certain that all your statuory rights are known, and met. This does not mean you have to turn into a harridan, but it does involve reading all documents and printed matter relating to your job, and making sure everything is fair and legal, before you commit yourself to signing anything. There is a tendency to imagine that anything printed must be all right, but this is by no means always the case. Contracts can be very one-sided so, if you are not sure, ask to think it over and, if necessary, take advice. The EOC will advise you on the legality of a work contract.

There is no doubt that reading through the small print is boring, which is one reason why it is small – to put you off reading it. But it must be done at the outset, otherwise you may not have grounds for complaint later.

In these days, when unemployment is an ever-present threat, and hardly anyone's job remains secure, you need to be able to hang on to as many rights as possible, so never sign them away.

As a general rule of thumb, the longer you stay in the same job, the more rights you accrue. If you work 16 hours a week at least, with the same employer, you have the right to a written contract of employment, and an itemized pay statement that lists both your gross and net pay. It must also include any pension and National Insurance deductions. You also have the right to take paid time off work if you are a trade union official, and the right to take time off, without pay, for union activities.

As you continue to work for the same firm, you gradually acquire more rights. In general, the longer you have worked for the same company, the harder they will find it to sack you without having an extremely good reason. Most firms, when laying off staff, operate on a 'last in, first out' basis, and the law upholds this idea. Loyalty and commitment to a firm, should be rewarded, the law feels. If you flit from job to job, as women tend to do, especially when they are part-time workers, you may find you have hardly any rights at all, as you can't carry them on from the previous job and add them up, as it were.

After four weeks' service you have the right to a guarantee payment, if you are suddenly laid off without warning. The Department of Employment will have the current rates of what this guarantee payment should be, but it is based on your weekly earnings. It may not, though, amount to the whole of your weekly wage. Also, after a month's service, you become entitled to your pay even if you are suspended on medical grounds. A month in the job entitles you, in addition, the right to a minimum period of notice. In other words, you can't be told to get out, without pay, that minute.

After 26 weeks, or six months in the same job, you earn the right to a written statement from your employers giving full reasons, if they decide they want to dismiss you. After one year, you then have the right not to be unfairly dismissed.

When you have given two years full-time, or five years part-time service in the same job, you then qualify for maternity leave, and the right to return. This right may not apply in very small firms, particularly if the total staff is fewer than five.

When you land a job, you may be asked to sign a contract setting out the terms and conditions of the job. Never sign a contract until you have had time to digest its contents properly. The conditions laid down in the contract should be legal and fair, and take into account any recent changes in the employment laws. If you are not certain whether the contract is fair, you can take it to your local Job Centre and ask them to have a look at it.

If your firm has a trade union representative, and you are a member of the relevant union, he or she would also have a look at your contract before you sign, and advise you accordingly.

Dismissal is a highly contentious and difficult subject, and if you claim you have been unfairly sacked, this is very likely to be hotly contested by your employer, who may try to say you resigned of your own accord. As a general rule, try never to resign, even if you are boiling over with rage. Women can often feel that the easy way out of a tricky situation at work is to walk out of the door and never return, but this means you lose all the rights you may otherwise possess. Whenever you possibly can, stand your ground and allow the firm to sack you. It may seem more dignified to resign, and certainly it will give you short-term satisfaction, but dignity does not pay the rent, and the only one who loses in the long run is you.

It is particularly important never to resign after a row, or out of pique. If your employer does give you notice to leave, first check that he is legally entitled to do so. Go straight to your union representative, if you have one, and see what your legal position is. You are normally entitled to one week's notice for every year of service but, in your first year, you are allowed one week's notice in any event.

This notice build-up stops after 12 years, but your employer can always ask you to take pay in lieu of notice. Often this works out for the best as, by the time it comes to a parting of the ways, relations have very often become less than cordial.

You can be dismissed there and then, without pay or notice, for gross misconduct. But what is this? Again, it depends very much on individual definition. Those who are caught with their hands in the till, or blatantly fiddling company accounts, usually will not have a case against dismissal. If you have been 'borrowing' money from, say, the firm's social club account, and fully intend to pay it back, you may be all right.

Breaking a fundamental company rule usually counts as gross misconduct, if you have signed a contract saying you will abide by this rule, on joining the firm. For example, a large company may have a rule that employees are not allowed to accept free gifts from commercial organizations. One company I worked for had such a rule. When a senior employee was found to be breaking the rule, by accepting free gifts worth many hundreds of pounds, he was dismissed on the spot. He took his case to ACAS, but they ruled that his boss was well within his rights to dismiss the employee in this way.

It is probably true to say, in any large company, there is no such thing as complete fair play. What counts as gross misconduct for one employee may not even be noticed for another. Very much depends on whether the company actually wants to go on employing you. But generally speaking, if you like the firm and they like you, you are unlikely to commit acts of gross misconduct, nor will they attempt to accuse you of them.

Making love behind the filing cabinets may or may not count as misconduct serious enough to warrant dismissal. This is a very tricky area indeed. If a couple persist in canoodling in office hours, they can probably be handed their cards. But if the 'offence' occurs long after the day's work has been concluded, the loving pair may be able to get off with a warning. It is unlikely that this conduct would be a case for instant dismissal, unless repeated warnings had gone unheeded.

In theory, you cannot be dismissed on grounds of ill health, though chronic or persistent illness may justify an eventual sacking. There is no clear-cut definition of how long a boss would have to wait, so we can only go on the decisions of industrial tribunals in this matter in the past.

The tribunals always have to ask certain questions. Could the boss reasonably have waited longer before handing the employer her cards? How long has the employee been in the job, and has there been a good general record of service? What effect is the illness likely to have on the job, both now and in the future? Will somebody else have to be employed, while the worker in question is off sick?

However ill you are, you can't be sacked just like that. The company you work for must have monitored your condition carefully, and this could mean your having to undergo a medical examination organized by them. A refusal to abide by this could constitute grounds for dismissal. A fair-minded firm will be prepared to discuss the illness with you, and try to see whether suitable alternative work can be arranged. You have to remember, though, that no company has a legal obligation to arrange lighter, more part-time work at your previous level of pay.

You can probably be sacked for smoking at work if the company has a non-smoking rule, so long as you have been given prior warning that persistent smokers could now face the sack.

Unfair dismissal comes about when your boss breaks an important term of the contract. But play this carefully, as a refusal to abide by the new terms could be interpreted as resignation. If you are demoted, or removed to another department, you have to make it clear in writing that you are not resigning, and that you regard your boss's heavy-handed action as 'constructive dismissal'. There are two ways open for those who consider themselves to be unfairly dismissed: asking for your old job back, or demanding compensation.

The latter course tends to be far more popular. You can be compensated only for those losses you can actually prove, plus any potential redundancy money you may have accumulated. You should make your unfair dismissal claims on Form ITI, available from your nearest Unemployment Benefit Office. Usually, your hearing will come up between six and eight weeks after filing the ITI.

Before proceeding with an unfair dismissal claim, you have to consider seriously whether it would be worth it. The claim itself will take a lot of time, trouble, and heartache and, at the end, even if you win, you may be able to claim only a few hundred pounds. A very high proportion of unfair dismissal payouts are for less than £1,000. The eventual amount you are awarded takes into account your age, length of service, likelihood of getting another job, and whether you are still unemployed months later, when the case is actually heard.

The claim is probably worth persisting with if the firm you have been working with makes a practice of sacking its employees unfairly. But once you get known for bringing a case, you could get yourself a bad name on the job circuit. This tends to happen in small places, and is unlikely to be a problem in a large city. But vengeful behaviour does have a way of sneaking up on people, and very often it can be best to let bygones be bygones. It may be wiser for you just to forget a bad boss, using the valuable experience you have gained to put you more on your guard with future employers.

Pensions are a difficult subject at any time, but more particularly so for women. Though there has been talk of making a common retiring age of 63, nothing has come of it so far. One problem is that pensions are excluded from the scope of the Equal Opportunities Commission so, however unfair it all seems, there is very little you can do about it at present. Pensions are handled by the Occupational Pensions Board, and they do discriminate against women, there is no doubt of it.

As a woman, you are extremely likely to lose out as regards pensions. This happens because women tend to be in workforce for shorter periods than men, are more likely to do part-time work and, anyway, do not have equal pension rights, even when their job description and status is equal to a male worker in the same occupation. Usually, the small print on your pension agreement sets out everything you need to know, but very few people ever read it. The situation is complicated still further if your firm makes joining its own scheme a condition of your employment with them. Firms are quite entitled to do this, and you can't then opt out of their pension scheme to join a private one of your own.

One leading female consultant surgeon at a London teaching hospital found, after reading her pension scheme regulations, that her husband and children would get no money whatsoever if she died while at work. Yet a man in the same position, paying an identical amount into an identical pension fund, would be able to provide for his wife and children. On the death of a husband a wife would normally be entitled to a widow's pension. But a man is not entitled to a widower's pension.

The pension set-up assumed that the woman is financially dependent on the man, even if she is the main breadwinner. The only thing you can do here, if you find yourself in this position, is to take out an extra, private insurance policy to safeguard your family. The consultant surgeon said: 'I'm having to pay into two schemes to get exactly the same benefit as a male consultant.' As she is employed by the NHS, and joining the pension scheme was a condition of her employment, she could not opt out. Also, the retiring age in this case was identical for men and women, so there was no logical reason at all why male and female consultants should not be treated as pensionable equals.

As a general rule, if you pay National Insurance Contributions, you are entitled to a state pension. You can have these payments credited to you if you like, while you are studying or bringing up children. It all depends on how you view your eventual pension. There is a lot of talk about how badly off pensioners are in this country, but statistics completely disprove this. The editor of the pre-retirement magazine *Choice*, said the magazine was flourishing because people now had a lot of money to spend, and so the magazine could attract a lot of advertising. The old people's holiday company *SAGA*, is one of the most successful travel firms in the country and, in its annual report, marvelled at the way old people now travelled all over the world.

It is not a good idea to worry too much about your pension. You will often see highly persuasive advertisements urging you to take out vast insurance policies to protect you in your old age, but you also have to consider whether you could better use the money now. People who are badly off tend to be those who have only their state pension to live on, but even here, supplementary benefit is available, so there is still no absolute need to worry. Also, old people have many concessions, on travel, at hairdressers, and places of entertainment. Don't be tempted to make yourself hard-up in your early years, just to ensure comfort in old age.

Apart from the state pension, many, though by no means all, employers offer additional pension schemes, and these are calculated on the highest paid years of your working life. If your company is a large one, it may offer a company scheme of its own, and this entitles you to contract out of the state additional scheme. Your NI contributions will be reduced accordingly, as you would now be paying in all your pension contributions to your employer's scheme.

If you think you will be with your present firm for a number of years, you would almost certainly do better by opting out of the state scheme. Part-timers may be excluded from company schemes and, generally, women do less well than men all along the line where pensions are concerned. Women tend to change jobs more often, and this in itself could be seriously detrimental to your eventual pension. In fact, somebody who changes jobs four times in 40 years could end up with a pension of less than half of somebody who stayed in the same job until retirement. This could be the case even though the contributions might be identical. The present schemes also militate against women, as the eventual pension is calculated on pay at retirement, and older women are far less likely to be promoted than older men. In fact, older women could find themselves being demoted as retirement approaches.

If you want to take up a lighter, part-time job as you get older, you could find yourself discriminated against on this account, pension-wise.

The National Consumer Council have now drawn up some recommendations to alter the present iniquitous pension scheme structure, which it thinks stems mainly from the monopoly of those companies providing pensions. The NCC feels that employees should be free to choose a personal pension scheme rather than have to pay into a group occupational scheme. Any reputable insurance company will be only too glad to outline its various pension schemes to you, but shop around before you decide. Employees, recommends the NCC, should receive a proper prospectus of the types of scheme in existence, and then make an informed choice on which they prefer. If the personal scheme is better, they should be able to contract out of the company scheme. And don't forget that paying into a company pension scheme provides a lot of cash for that company to invest in the meantime.

A recent change in the law has given a slightly better pension deal to those who change their jobs. The system of 'franking', whereby companies can pay reduced pensions to those who change their jobs, has now been abolished.

If a worker spends more than five years in an occupational pension scheme which is contracted out of the state earnings-related scheme, then she cannot have a refund of her pension when she leaves, The pension money so far paid in must either be kept for her in the scheme, or transferred to the new employer, or put into a special 'transfer' pension scheme with an insurance company. The whole thing is horrendously complicated, but the employer must guarantee the part of the pension which is replacing the state scheme. The guarantee is that the employer, instead of the state, will pay this amount, so that the employee should not lose out.

The new anti-franking clauses in the Health and Social Security Bill, brought into force in May, 1984, are designed to ensure that the extra pension you may have earned is paid, on top of the amount employers guarantee.

Self-employed people are able to claim tax relief for personal pension schemes. It is worth discussing this with your accountant. Sorry to sound cynical here, but many firms of accountants are often wooed by insurance companies who give them a rake-off for selling certain schemes to their clients. Beware if your accountant tries a little too hard to push a particular scheme onto you. This is all, unfortunately, accepted business practice, and may catch you unawares, so do be on your guard.

If you are a self-employed woman in business in a small town, you will find that bank managers, accountants, male businessmen, all tend to belong to Rotary Clubs or Freemasons, from which women are excluded. In theory, this should not affect your rights, but it may mean you have to be extra careful who you deal with. You are unlikely to find, in any town, an alternative team of women bank managers, accountants, and so on, whom you can use instead, more's the pity. It is a sad fact of working life that, whereas men club together, women on the whole don't, and secret and semi-secret organizations are very much part of the business world. This should not affect your rights, but it could.

Redundancy
Redundancy is always a possibility, unless you are running your own business. You never know when a company might have a 'rationalization' scheme, or decide you are no longer economically viable as an employee, or perhaps go out of business altogether.

If you have been working full-time, that is, 16 hours a week or more, for over a month, you cannot be made redundant without pay or notice. Those who are made redundant should be entitled to a lump sum payment, so long as they have been working for the same employer for more than two years. Some people, such as those on fixed term contracts, National Health Service workers, or those employed outside the UK, may not be entitled to this sum.

You will, though, automatically lose your right to redundancy pay if you are on strike when you receive your notice. Suppose you were not on strike, and working properly at the time, you should get a final payment based on the following rather complicated calculations. You have to add together one week's pay for every year between your 22nd and 41st birthday, one-and-a-half weeks' pay between your 18th and 22nd birthdays, assuming you have been working for the same company that long. You can't add up birthdays before you joined the firm, and expect them to count in your favour. £145 a week is the maximum that can be taken into account when calculating redundancy pay, and only the last 20 years' employment.

Redundancy payments are usually tax-free up to £25,000, but if you continue to work during your notice period, this will be taxed in the usual way.

You may be asked, instead of redundancy payments, to accept

alternative work within the same firm. You must take this, so long as the job is suitable for you. But you could refuse, and still be eligible for redundancy money, if the job entails moving to another part of the country, is at very much lower pay, or has very different working hours.

Sometimes, firms will try to get away with paying far less redundancy money than they should. In fact, this is a common ploy. Here you have several possible means of redress, you can seek advice from your trade union, Citizens' Advice Bureau, Job Centre, Unemployment Benefit Office or solicitor. If you want to take your case to an industrial tribunal, this must be done within six months of the redundancy notice being served.

You may feel that being made redundant isn't quite fair if, for example, other people who have worked for the company for a shorter time are being kept on. Here you could have a good case against the firm that seeks to dismiss you.

Perhaps your company has gone bust, and you are told there is simply no money in the kitty to pay any redundancy. When this happens, you should write at once to the Department of Employment, as they administer a redundancy fund especially for this kind of eventuality. You may need to contact the liquidator or receiver to get back any pay, holiday entitlement, or redundancy money that should be due to you. You can claim these from the Central Redundancy Fund, and may get up to eight weeks' salary, or six weeks' holiday pay.

Sick pay
Sick pay rates are divided into various bands of earnings, with sick pay covering between just over a half to over three-quarters of your normal wage. This is currently up to a ceiling earning level of £68, over which you will not get more than £42.25 sick pay. And if you earn less than £34, you are excluded from sick pay rates altogether. The daily rate for sick pay is the appropriate weekly rate divided by the number of qualifying days in the week, starting with Sunday, in which the day to be paid occurs.

Unemployment benefit
This is the current situation regarding unemployment benefit or 'the dole'. You can claim for this if you have been paying Class I National Insurance contributions and are capable of and available for work. You cannot claim if you are a married woman and have been paying the lower married woman's contribution. This stopped in 1977, but some older women workers may still be paying it, and it excludes you from benefit. Class 2 contributions, as paid by self-employed people, do not

count for unemployment benefit. Leaflet NL 12 explains all the ins and outs.

You will not be eligible for unemployment benefit for a period of up to six weeks if you lose your job through misconduct. Otherwise, you will be able to claim straightaway, as soon as you are out of work. Many married women imagine that they are not entitled to unemployment benefit, as they tend to confuse this with supplementary benefit. But even if your husband is continuing to work, you will be able to claim if you have paid in the relevant contributions. After all, it is your money – you are not taking it away from anybody else. Nor do you become ineligible after having a baby, provided you continue to look for work, and have not let your contributions get out of date.

Other women may not consider signing on, especially if they have been working part-time, because they automatically assume less than full-time work will exclude them from unemployment benefit. In fact, so many eligible women all over the country are not signing on, that campaigns are now being started up in several areas to persuade and encourage them to do so.

The general position is that any woman who has worked between this April and the last April, and has earned more than £675 as well as paying full NI contributions, is entitled to some benefit. It may not be the full amount, though. The smallest amount you can claim is £12.50 a week and the maximum £25. It's not exactly a fortune, but a worthwhile weekly amount even so, especially while you are looking for work. Also, it may entitle you to other benefits, such as cheap sports facilities in your area.

But you do have to be serious about looking for work. The money is not available for women who just want to sit at home. As the situation stands at present, if you have worked for at least 24 weeks during the past two years, you are entitled to sign on. But you can't suddenly sign on after spending five years at home not earning, however much you may have paid in the past. If you haven't worked for several years, these sums just go down the drain, and are lost for ever.

Those who have been working part-time, and get laid off, must think very seriously about whether they want to return to work. If you do decide to look for another part-time job, you will have to fill in a different form. For example, if you say you are willing to work three days a week, you would get three days' benefit, which is £4 a day, at present rates. But if you can only obtain part-time work, when you are willing and able to work full-time, then you might be entitled to unemployment benefit for the days when you are not working.

If you would like preliminary advice on this, the Citizens' Advice

Bureau will be able to tell you what to do. Or you can contact your local centre for the unemployed, if there is one in your area.

You can collect unemployment benefit for one year, after which this kind of benefit stops.

Sexual harassment

There is no actual law covering sexual harassment, but one or two cases on the subject have been brought to industrial tribunals. In one, a garage boss grabbed a girl's cashier's legs, tried to undo her blouse and put his hand inside her bra. He followed her into the toilet, then picked her up and threw her onto the showroom floor. He may have regarded all this as a jolly jape, but she decided she wasn't amused, and threatened to tell his wife about his behaviour. The boss responded by sacking his employee.

In another very similar case, a girl threw a glass of lager over her boss at a firm's party when he tried to put his hands down her dress. She was later sacked as well. The industrial tribunals in both cases ruled that the treatment of the young women amounted to unfair sex discrimination. They were, the tribunal decided, treated less favourably solely because of their sex, and were awarded sums of £1,343 and £2,255 respectively, plus a small sum in each case to compensate for injured feelings and loss of dignity.

Anybody who has to leave her job, or who is sacked because of not responding to sexual harassment, can bring a case under the Sex Discrimination Act. But you would have to be able to prove the harassment, and the case could well go against you. In matters like this, it can be very difficult to know in advance how the tribunal will feel.

In one now famous case, three women who worked for Mirror Group Newspapers complained that they were physically and verbally harassed after they had joined the previously all-male trade union Sogat '82. The women settled for £100 compensation each, and a guarantee that they would be hassled no more.

The Equal Opportunities Commission can give advice on cases of sexual harassment, and it is worth consulting them before proceeding with any legal form of redress. You have to play matters like these very carefully indeed, as you can easily find yourself labelled a trouble-maker, and this could be bad news for your future career. There is a certain type of employee, and it is not confined to sex, who is always complaining about unfair treatment at work, and who always seem to be hard done by. Sexual harassment cases tend to lead to ribald jokes as well. Male employees are only too likely to say things like: 'Sexual harassment? You can come and sexually harass me any time you like.' If you're attractive, the attitude of the other employees is liable to be that you've asked for it, and if you are plain, they will tend to think it's all wishful thinking. So a lot of detailed thinking is needed before rushing to bring any case of alleged sexual harassment to the courts.

It is also true that most of those sitting on an industrial tribunal will be men, and that those with power in the workplace will also be men. It is always easier to fire a secretary than the managing director, and you could be accused of making it all up. A survey conducted by the secretarial agency Alfred Marks revealed that 53 per cent of those troubled by sexual harassment at work changed their jobs rather than publicly complaining about their treatment.

Part-time work

As we've seen, part-time workers have far fewer rights than those who work full-time. This could be construed as indirect discrimination against women, as about 90 per cent of part-time workers are women. Very often, part-time work is all that women can get, but if you possibly can make it up to a full-time job – at least enough to win yourself some employment rights – then please do. Many firms like to keep as many part-time workers as possible, to avoid having to treat them like full-time staff. As a part-timer, you must work for five years before qualifying for redundancy money, as against two years if you are a full-time worker. To be eligible for any rights at all, you must have a contract of service, as opposed to a contract *for services*. The first means that you are employed, but the second means that you are counted as being self-employed, and are actually a freelance operator.

It may sound like a small distinction, but it could be crucial. Those who are on a fixed salary will usually be regarded as employees, whereas women who are paid piece rates will most often be self-employed. If you are offered part-time work, make sure you know whether this gives you employee, as opposed to self-employed, status. If you work mainly for other people, you will be far better off with self-employed status, though this can be harder to achieve.

It is often being said that women are going to come into their own with new technology, as this can be done in the home, and you won't even have to go out to work. But a report published in May, 1984 showed that women were not benefitting at all, financially, from this technology, as it just gave another excuse for mothers at home to be paid low levels.

In one study, commissioned by the Equal Opportunities Commission, it was found that pay levels were nearly £2 an hour lower for those working at home than for women properly employed in offices, doing exactly the same job. Homeworkers who were skilled computer professionals were earning on average £4.63 an hour, compared to £6.54 an hour for identical work done by similarly qualified people in an office.

The moral here is plain: don't take on freelance home-based work if you can help it, as you could find yourself without any rights at all. Nearly all homeworkers are women, and most of these are mothers tied to the house with young children, or disabled people. Most homeworkers do all their work for the same company, but are considered self-employed. This means that if no work comes in for many weeks, there is nothing you can do about it – you just don't get paid anything. Homeworkers should always stick out for employment status. Never let yourself be so desperate that you accept work from companies who pay you only on casual rates, at least for any length of time.

In the past, firms have tended to take great advantage of women working at home. As they are isolated from other workers they can't easily compare their conditions with other home workers, or even office workers. There is a huge difference between homeworking for just one company and running your own business. In the former, you have all the disadvantages without having any benefits at all. Even the money you earn will be paltry.

It is possible to work at home and still have employment status. The survey showed that those of the sample of 78 new technology workers who had the rights and status of employed people were better off all along the line. Their employment status entitled them to holiday pay, maternity and sickness, and they also earned on average 30 per cent more than those who were considered to be self-employed. More than that, they enjoyed far greater job security, as they could not just be laid off at a moment's notice.

There are now over three million working women in this country whose jobs involve processing information. Many of these could quite easily work at home, but anybody who is considering opting for this should make sure they will continue with their employed status. Self-employed sounds nice, perhaps, but it's a nonsense if you remain tied to one firm. The trouble again is the old one: so many women tend to be so grateful for being offered any work at all, especially work that fits in with domestic commitments, that they will accept low pay and dreadful conditions. It all comes about through not valuing yourself enough as a human being, something women are notoriously prone to. Once you realize that you have an important, even vital, place in the workforce, this realization in itself can make you put a higher value on your own services. The higher your skills are, the more value you have, so if you are a woman worker in any kind of new technology, make sure you get a reasonable deal from your firm.

Making sure of your rights takes vigilance, and needs constant attention, but if you don't ensure all your rights are being met, nobody else will.

Further Reading

The New Homeworkers, Ursula Huws (Low Pay Unit, 1984).
Maternity Rights: the Experience of Employers, W. W. Daniel (the Policy Studies Institute, 1981).
The Which? Guide to Your Rights (Consumers Association, 1980).

8

Your Salary

It is a sad fact that, for every £100 a man earns, a woman earns on average £60. This is in spite of the Equal Pay Act, the Sex Discrimination Act and, theoretically at least, equal opportunities in education. Women still tend to be concentrated in the lower paid professions such as the textile and food industries, clerical and nursing work, and junior level teaching.

But that is not the only reason why women receive less pay for the work they do than men. After all, as Shakespeare said, 'what is aught but as 'tis valued?' Women may be mainly in the lower paid professions, but it is also true to say that these jobs are lower paid because women are in them.

Women receive lower salaries than men because they have not learned to fight for themselves in the financial jungle. When it comes to asking for more money, we women are so nervous of fighting on our own behalf that we put up with derisory pay levels, and conditions that few men would entertain for a minute.

We go on putting up with less because we don't like to ask for more. But if we do want to earn more, it's no use waiting for 'them' to negotiate on our behalf. The whole point of the market economy, as we have got in this country, is to use the cheapest labour that will do the job. If no women would accept £1.50 an hour for cleaning, and all over the country demanded £10 an hour, they'd get it, if people wanted clean houses and offices. But nobody possessing the merest smattering of business sense is going to pay more than they have to, for anything. Women's labour comes cheaper than men's, so with all those services that nobody wants to pay vast sums for, women are wheeled in to do the jobs.

Any woman who is anxious to earn a decent salary must learn how to fight for herself in the financial jungle. We must learn how to negotiate for ourselves, and win ourselves a greater share of the salary cake. Most men know, in their hearts, that they are not really worth more than we are for the jobs they do, but they have been more aggressive at demanding higher wages.

In writing this chapter, I am deeply indebted to the only book on the subject of women's salaries that I have ever come across in this country, and it is written by an American woman, Sherry Chastain. I shall pass on her invaluable advice, as it contains many tips that we could all use in the business of getting more money for ourselves.

The basic problem with women, according to Sherry Chastain, and I agree with her, is that they find it deeply embarrassing to talk about money. This is happening partly because we are so new to the game of earning money for ourselves, as in the past being 'feminine' meant not to know anything about filthy lucre. When the lady's way of being clever with money was to get some rich man to support her, there was not much point in knowing about negotiating and bargaining for better pay levels. Nowadays, though, any girl worth her salt would prefer to support herself.

But she won't be able to do this very well until she has learned how to bargain on her own behalf. And this *doesn't* mean becoming a nasty, ruthless, money-grabbing sort of person. It simply means refusing to accept less than is your due on the market place.

Women often fear asking for more money because they think that going in and asking for a rise will result in them being handed their cards instead. You hear women saying things like, 'I daren't ask for more, I'm a single parent and I've got my children to support.' Or, 'I daren't ask for more as if I lose this job I'll never get another one.' It is fact that women who work 'just for the money' as opposed to women who work because they love their jobs and want to thrive in their careers, are always the lowest paid. In the OPCS 1984 survey: *Women and Employment: A Lifetime Perspective*, where several thousand women were interviewed about their jobs, most of the part-time, unskilled workers gave as their chief reason for working, 'money for essentials'. *Yet most of them were hardly earning anything at all: £29 a week was an average amount.* And these days, £29 a week doesn't buy many essentials.

So many women daren't take a chance on losing even a low paid job. It's this attitude that keeps those who employ female homeworkers on starvation rates in business.

It is true that winning yourself a better salary will always involve taking risks. I once worked for a magazine that was run, very badly, on a shoestring. I took the job because, at the time, it was the only one I could get, and soon found myself doing most of the work for hardly any money. When I mentioned, nervously, the question of a rise, the next thing I knew, I was being handed my cards. It was the last job I ever took at paltry pay. The experience taught me to value myself more, and to demand a decent level (or *request* it, I should say: you can't actually demand a high salary of those who might employ you).

Having said that, you must be aware of your market value. You can't expect to earn high amounts if you are unskilled, inexperienced and extremely young. You are very likely to be exploited at first. But there is a difference between a youngster still wet behind the ears being paid a tiny wage, and a 50-year-old woman still being expected to exist on hardly anything.

When I asked for a higher salary at the magazine, I knew I was taking a risk. After all, I had been glad enough to get the job at the time. But I soon got a very much better job, with a newspaper, and wasn't out of work for long at all. There are two possible ways of regarding risks. One is the negative approach, which is concerned only with what you might lose. The other is the positive approach, which considers instead what you stand to gain. Almost anybody who has ever made real money for themselves has done it by taking risks – and by no means does every gamble always pay off.

The first rule in successful negotiation – and this applies to more than just money – is to avoid direct confrontation. Many women sit at their desks seething with indignation because they know they are being underpaid, or because they have just found out that a man in a lesser position is actually earning more, or has a company car, or some other perk that indicates he is valued more highly. This was me – once. In one of my jobs, I was supposed to be on equal footing with the male employees, yet most of them had a company car, and I didn't. Nor did any of the other female employees at my level. In the end, after writhing with indignation and shame, I went to my boss and confronted him. He simply took no notice of my threats and I still didn't get a company car. Instead of presenting proper arguments, I took the it's-not-fair, self-pitying approach, and it was a completely ineffectual way to handle the situation.

Sherry Chastain says that women in offices tend to behave like spoilt children when they go and ask for more money. They get hot under the collar, rant and rave and stamp their feet, and it gets them nowhere. Instead of getting cross, you must remain firm but even-tempered. It is up to you to teach your employer that you are actually worth more money for what you are doing. The best way to do this is to point out, positively and with specific examples, how valuable you are and have been to the company. You must also actually know how much you are worth. This involves doing some homework, and discovering how much others doing similar jobs are getting, not just in your own company, but in comparable firms. You should also find out what fringe benefits and perks, if any, are applicable in your case.

When applying for a new job, or a higher salary for the same job, do have a definite figure in mind for yourself. Go into the interview knowing exactly what you expect to achieve. Also, keep a mental note all the time of how much you are prepared to accept for the job, and don't go lower than this figure. Sometimes an employer might say: 'We'll see that you're all right', and you may take this to mean he will be extremely generous. But his idea of all right may not be yours – so ask him to lay it on the line and say how much he is prepared to pay you. This isn't being aggressive – simply businesslike, and bosses will admire you for it.

If the employer objects to the price you are putting on yourself, ask yourself why, but never assume that because he won't meet your demands, you are not worth any more.

You must always know the range of salaries that are being paid to people in your position, offering similar skills and with similar experience, and this will help you to put a realistic price on yourself.

If you are a school leaver with just two CSEs, you can't expect a five figure salary. But even if you are a raw recruit, going after your first job, don't just assume that your prospective employer, who may have years and years of experience at employing people just like yourself, will automatically know how much he should be paying you. He will, if he follows the pattern of most employers, be attempting to get you for the lowest possible price. Find out exactly what salary scales are being paid for your kind of work by looking in relevant trade journals and magazines. Ask around, ask friends, and others with similar qualifications and experience what they are getting.

Most salary negotiations involve lengthy contact between employer and employee. When discussing your possible remuneration, remember to look him straight in the eye. If you keep avoiding eye contact, this makes you seem either shifty or unduly nervous. A straight and level gaze, the so-called 'business gaze' where you keep your eyes focused on the triangle between his eyes and to a place just above, on his forehead, in itself makes you seem sensible and serious. Don't fix him with a hypnotic stare. Your job is to win him over to your point of view, not to unnerve him. Sit straight on your chair, don't fold your arms, and don't use hand-to-face gestures if you can help it. These can make you seem as if you are using some kind of deception. Keep your arms loosely to your side, and your legs together, crossed perhaps at the ankle, but not at the knee, which makes you look defensive. Sit back in your chair and don't lean forward. The boss will have the advantage, probably, of sitting behind a big desk and in a swivel chair, which always looks more imposing. But if you remember the 'business gaze' this will help to even up the situation somewhat.

When the employer starts talking, stop whatever you are saying to listen carefully. Hear him out, and never interrupt. As soon as he has finished, allow a little time for silence to elapse – this will make you seem more in control – then outline your points. Do not, when you go in for interview, convey the impression that you are prepared to accept a low salary. Neither should you rush to accept an employer's initial offer of a small salary, because you want the job so much. If applying for a new job, you must give the impression that you are not prepared to join the firm unless the financial compensation is adequate. They must want to employ *you*, not the other way round. Otherwise, if you let them think you will love them for ever if they deign to take you on, you are negotiating yourself a tiny wage before you start.

Initially, always ask for more than you expect to get. Women are notoriously bad at this. You can back down from a too-high figure, but can never recover from a low one. Don't imagine that if you put a low price on yourself, the employer will rush to better it. Rather, he will be delighted to have got you so cheaply, and will even boast about it to his colleagues. A friend of mine, who launched his own art materials business, loves to point out how cheaply he gets his women employees. And they are all graduates, too, he will tell you. Some from Oxford. He employs mainly women, not because he prefers them, or thinks they work harder or anything, but simply because they are cheaper. He knows that if he advertises a job at a certain (low) salary, only women will apply. Even just after they have left university, men tend to put a higher value on themselves.

Women can mistakenly feel that lowering their price will improve their chances of landing a job, but this is bad psychology. You should be far more inclined to play hard to get, as this automatically increases your value. If the employer offers you a salary, then implies that you must take it or leave it because it's the very best he can do, you may feel that the game is over and that you have lost. But not necessarily. If you truly want the job, but only if, ask for a salary rise in three months' time. And, during all of that three months, continue to offer additional proof of your potential value to your employer. Always act as though you will get what you want.

It's not necessary, when going for interview, to wrap everything up on the same day. Ask for time to think, as this won't jeopardise your chances of getting the job. Then you can ask around, find out what the going rates are, and come back with enquiries about fringe benefits, pension schemes or other perks that might go with the job. Whenever you are asked how much money you had in mind, give a definite figure. For example, if you have discovered, by judicious research, that someone in your position should be getting £9,250, say so, rather than: I thought between £9,000 and £10,000.

A question women often find difficult to answer, but one that is almost always asked is: what were you earning before? Dishonesty is never the best policy, but a previous low salary can trap you into long-term low earnings. There are two possible approaches here. You can either be absolutely direct and say straight out, £4,500. Or, a better way is to say: 'I will be earning £5,250 by the end of the year'. *Never* give your correct salary, then add: 'but I was underpaid'. This suggests that you are weak and complaining, and will not endear a potential employer to you. If, like so many women, you have been doing voluntary work, find out what you would have got if the job was paid.

The employer may tell you he has other good candidates to interview. Well, so he might, but don't be put off by this. That's his problem, not yours, so you can just carry on quietly, but firmly, without backing down in any way.

He may say that, if you accept the job, three months after you have been taken on you will become eligible for luncheon vouchers, a car, expenses, or whatever. If he says this, it will be up to you to remind him of his promise when three months have elapsed. You can't expect him to remember, and he won't. If you feel nervous of negotiating in this grown-up way, don't let your fears stop you. *Bear in mind that you have nothing whatever to lose.* Don't ever take on board the idea that to be bold is unfeminine. This attitude is outdated in the jobs world, and it will never get you anywhere.

Another problem holding many women back from decent pay is the concept of loyalty to their firm. Clever bosses can be very adept at making a woman feel needed and indispensable, without ever digging into her pockets, or putting their money where their mouth is. Never, ever, become hampered by misguided feelings of loyalty. If they want you that much, they must be prepared to pay you what you are worth.

It is possible, that you may have to leave your present firm in order to achieve a higher salary. Moving around is usually a good way of getting on, and you do improve your salary every time you change jobs. Or you should, otherwise there is little point in leaving.

What if you get the job then discover, too late, that you are being paid far less than others? If this happens, go straight in and see your boss, not to complain, but to offer a proposal which will increase your worth to the company. A firm will usually find a way of paying what you ask, but only if it can be convinced you are worth it. It is up to you to convince them that you are.

Always try to dissociate yourself from what you are doing in the job world. While giving of your best, remain detached from it all. And don't expect that you will win every battle. Even Julius Caesar didn't win every war he waged, and neither did anybody else. However powerful and influential people are, they never come off victorious every single time. If you accept this, but don't take it as an indication that you are no good generally, you will win in the end.

It may be extremely difficult to negotiate in jobs where there are very fixed salaries, such as government jobs, teaching or medicine. But even here, there are usually ways round. You can start by applying for a job at a higher grade than you hope to get. Those who eventually achieve high salaries in public service jobs keep applying for better jobs and better positions. It is always worth applying, even if you don't reckon you have much chance, on the basis that you can't win a raffle if you don't first buy a ticket.

Through applying, you may get an opportunity to make a new and valuable contact, or you may be referred to somebody else who has an opening. Or you may be impressive that an opening is especially created for you. All these things have happened, and you will get bolder and better, the more you trust yourself to take the salary game into your own hands.

If there is one thing that marks high fliers out from others, it is that they are never afraid to take on a job that has high specifications. Ambitious people are always prepared to put in extra work to get on top of the job, even if this means going to evening classes, staying late at work, talking to new contacts out of hours. In order to take, you have to learn how to give, and if you are grudging you will never win yourself a high salary.

You may say, after reading this far: yes, I know it makes sense, but it's not me. I know I could never be like this. If this is the case, you may find there are others to do it for you. Join a union, in the first instance, if there is one applicable to your job. One organizing officer for NALGO (National and Local Government Officers Association) said: 'When I was a secretary 20 years ago, you never dreamed you could climb up the ladder. If you went in a secretary, that's what you stayed. But now that women are joining unions, things are at least getting better. It's easier for women to negotiate together because there's more at stake than when you are just bargaining on your own behalf. You don't feel so insulted if you don't get what you want, either. Also, I think you do a better job when you are going in for others. And, if you are a member of a union, you can take action when you run into difficulties with the management. This can be difficult if you are on your own.'

Here is one woman's experience of promotion gained by her own efforts. Verity is the buyer for three large departments in a major West

End store. She said: 'I came into the store training scheme after A-levels, and after one year, was promoted to assistant buyer in the men's toiletries and pharmacy departments. From the very first, I was determined to succeed in my chosen career, and I didn't mind working long hours, or on Saturdays, though it was at the expense of my social life.

'After I became an assistant buyer, I made sure the other buyers knew who I was and that I was very interested in my job. I soon realized that there was little possibility of my being promoted in the men's toiletries division, as the buyer there was a qualified pharmacist. Eventually, I was moved to the fashion floor, where I became assistant to the rainwear buyer. She was about to retire, as it happened, and had been asked to keep an eye on me. I had a good chance of becoming a buyer myself, I knew, if she gave me a favourable report.

'I made a big effort, and she gave me a good recommendation. So when she left I was made a buyer in my own right. You don't have to be pushy in an aggressive way to get promotion', Verity said. 'But you do have to make sure you are noticed. I also ensured that the figures I dealt with were absolutely correct. Sloppiness in these areas make bosses think you are a dumbo. I would double-check in my coffee break.'

A new little bit of legislation may help working women to get a slightly better deal, moneywise. Since January, 1984, the Equal Pay Act has been extended so that a woman can claim equal pay with a male colleague on the grounds that her work is of 'equal value' to his. This is an actual change in the law, designed to result in an increase in female earnings. Employers are also now being asked to introduce 'positive action' to make sure that women coming back after a career break to have children, are not automatically discriminated against. The OPCS report showed that the longer women take to come back after they have children, the lower their salaries.

The amended Equal Pay act would allow, for example, a female secretary to claim her work is of equal value to a male clerk working for the same employer. A woman machinist can claim that her work is of equal value to the work done by a male upholsterer.

But here, as in many other instances, the onus would be on you. You have to make the claim on your own behalf, and go to see the boss yourself. It is no use waiting around expecting 'them' to do it for you.

On a final note: you do have to realize that, however successful you may be in winning a large salary for yourself, however career minded you may be, it will actually cost you money to go out to work. Suppose you are a married woman earning £8,000. This gives you a gross income of £154 a week, but you may actually only be £82 a week better off. How so?

As a working wife, you will be accorded the wife's earned income allowance, which is the same as the single person's allowance, and currently £2,005 a year.

On this salary you and your husband would probably be taxed jointly, as with separate taxation, he would lose the married man's allowance. Then you have to deduct 30 per cent basic rate income tax, which leaves you with a net of £6,201. Then there is a National Insurance costing £720 a year (all 1984 figures). This sum assumes that you will be paying into the state pension scheme, rather than a firm's scheme. NI contributions are calculated as a percentage of your salary. At the moment, this is 9 per cent.

If you spend £2 a day getting to work, £220 a year on lunches, and another £60 on office whiprounds and the like, plus new clothes at £400 a year, this takes another £1,200 out of your income. All this means you have to deduct £3,718 from your annual salary of £8,000, which now leaves you £4,280 to play around with. As a single parent or widow, you would be entitled to more tax relief than this. The personal allowance for children is now worth £1,150, which you can add on to your personal tax relief of £2,005, making £3,155 of your income non-taxable.

All this may start to sound as if it's hardly worth going out to work. So much of your money will be draining out on compulsory deductions, which you can do absolutely nothing about. But these sums make you see how much you have to gain, and how little to lose, by playing the salary game. It is worth trying to increase the money you bring home, and the only real way of doing this is to earn more. The compulsory contributions don't go up much, so the more you earn, the better off you will be.

Yes, there is more to life than earning money, far more. But there is no reason why, just because you are a woman, you should be paid badly for the work you do.

Learn to value yourself more highly, learn to negotiate, and you will climb to the top of the salary tree. Good luck!

Further Reading

Winning the Salary Game, Salary Negotiation for Women, Sherry Chastain (John Wiley. 1980).

Moneylove, Jerry Gillies (Warner Books, 1981). This book explains how having a positive attitude towards money helps you to attract more of it into your life.

Index